Where Did the Reindeer Come From?

Alice Postell
at Sitka, Alaska

Where Did the Reindeer Come From?

Alaska Experience, the First Fifty Years

Alice Postell

AMAKNAK PRESS

PORTLAND, OREGON

Cover: Eskimo drawing, "Traveling with Reindeer,"
courtesy of National Archives.

"Rigorists," copyright © 1941, 1969 by Marianne Moore,
reprinted with permission of Macmillan Publishing Company.

Edited by Susan Page York.
Designed by John Laursen at Press-22.
Set in Meridien type by Irish Setter.
Map created by Al Cardwell.
Printed by Adprint Company.
Bound by Lincoln and Allen.
Manufactured in the United States of America.

Library of Congress Cataloging in Publication Data

Postell, Alice, 1910–
    Where did the reindeer come from?
    Alaska experience, the first fifty years.
    Bibliography: page 109
    Includes Index
    1. Eskimos—Alaska—Industries. 2. Reindeer industry
—Alaska. 3. Eskimos—Alaska—Economic conditions.
4. Jackson, Sheldon, 1834–1909. I. Title.
ISBN 0-9626090-0-5
E99.E7P64   1990   338.1'76294—dc20   90-146

Amaknak Press
13505 Southeast River Road
Portland, Oregon 97222

Dedicated to the Native Alaskan herders of reindeer
past, present, and future

Rigorists

"We saw reindeer
browsing," a friend who'd been in Lapland, said:
"finding their own food; they are adapted

to scant *reino*
or pasture, yet they can run eleven
miles in fifty minutes; the feet spread when

the snow is soft,
and act as show-shoes. They are rigorists,
however handsomely cutwork artists

of Lapland and
Siberia elaborate the trace
or middle-girth with saw-tooth leather lace.

One looked at us
with its firm face part brown, part white,—a queen
of alpine flowers. Santa Claus' reindeer, seen

at last, had gray-
brown fur, with a neck like edelweiss or
lion's foot,—*leontopodium* more

exactly." And
this candelabrum-headed ornament
for a place where ornaments are scarce, sent

to Alaska,
was a gift preventing the extinction
of the Eskimo. The battle was won

by a quiet man,
Sheldon Jackson, evangel to that race
whose reprieve he read in the reindeer's face.

Marianne Moore

Contents

Foreword   *R.N. DeArmond*   xiii

Acknowledgments   xv

Preface   xvii

Introduction   xix

Map of Alaska   xxii-xxiii

1   Early Alaska and the Ipani   3
    The Place   3
    The Ipani Way of Life   3

2   Tides of Change   7
    Early Outsiders   7
    Starting Government Schools   9

3   The Reindeer Project is Born   11
    An Idea Leads to Action   11
    Overcoming Early Challenges   12
    First Reindeer Purchase   15

4   An Industry Gets Under Way   16
    Teller Reindeer Station   16
    Schools and Herding Apprenticeships   17
    Early Problems   18

5   Lapp Herders Come to Alaska   22
    First Reindeer Superintendent   22
    The Lapps' Long Journey   23
    Lapp Teachers, Eskimo Apprentices   25

6   Reindeer Herds Multiply   26
    Charley Antisarlook's Herd   27
    Demand for Reindeer Services   27
    Reindeer Transport Troubles   27

7   The Rescue of Stranded Whalers   31
    Adapting the Rescue Plan   31
    Two Reindeer Herds   32
    Success   33
    New Reindeer Interest   35

8   Reindeer to Miners on the Yukon   36
    Overseas Organizing   36
    Another Long Journey   37
    Adjusting to Circumstances   39

9   Of Gold and Reindeer   40
    Nome Gold Rush   40
    Fleet-Footed Mail Service   42
    Eskimo Herd at Teller   43

10 A Growing Industry 44
    Events at Teller 44
    Eaton Succeeds Teller 44
    New Herds and Old 46
    Teller Properties Unprotected 46

11 Trials of Eskimos and Deer 47
    Gold Claims and Reindeer Ranges 47
    Epidemic 48
    Child in Snowdrift 49
    Tending the Reindeer Herds 49

12 The First Fifteen Years 53
    Standard Schools 53
    Industrial Schools and Hospitals 54
    Apprentice Training 55
    Planning for Chains of Stations 56
    Counting the Reindeer 57
    Keeping Track of Funds 57

13 Different Viewpoints 59
    Newcomers 59
    Churchill's Report 59
    A Matter of Opinion 60
    Evidence of Dissent 61

14 A New Era in the Reindeer Industry 63
    More Rules and Regulations 64
    Electoona, Okpolick, Seveck, Onalick 65
    A Surplus of Reindeer 65
    Lomen Enterprise 66
    First Major Sale to a Non-Native 67

15 Reindeer Fairs 69

16 Controversy 74
    Management of Eskimo Reindeer 74
    Lomen Marketing Efforts 76
    Continuing Problems 78

17 Conflicting Interests 79
    Grazing Rights and Ownership 79
    Further Lomen Marketing Efforts 80
    Eskimo Accomplishments Praised 81

18 Resolution 82
    Changing of the Guard 82
    Reindeer Council Ineffective 83
    Eskimo Leaders Speak Out 83
    Reindeer Act Restores Native Herds 85

Epilogue 86

Appendices
A Characteristics of Domestic Reindeer 90
B Reindeer Sled Ride 92
C Excerpt from the Daily Journal
    of Teller Reindeer Station 95
D Excerpts from Lopp's Diary
    on the Point Barrow Rescue 102

Endnotes 107

Bibliography 109

Index 113

Sidebars

Whales   4

Eskimo Art   10

Michael Healy   13

William T. Lopp   20

Nellie Kittredge Lopp   21

The Antisarlooks   32

An Uncommonly Severe Winter   39

Private Reindeer Enterprises   41

Emma Willoya   50

Herders and Their Reindeer   55

Roundups   57

Chester Asakak Seveck   66

Walter C. Shields   70

Clarence L. Andrews   75

Mackenzie River Drive   76

Foreword

Among the hundreds of individuals who traveled to Alaska during its first decade under the American flag, none had a greater impact on the new territory during the next thirty years than the Reverend Doctor Sheldon Jackson.

In addition to establishing Presbyterian churches and missions in many locations, he was one of the principal founders of a school that today bears his name as Sheldon Jackson College, built Alaska's first concrete building to house the Sheldon Jackson Museum, and brought the first reindeer from Siberia to Alaska for the benefit of the Eskimo people.

Dr. Jackson was small in physical stature —he stood barely more than five feet tall according to some accounts—but he was a giant when it came to getting things done. The first home of his school at Sitka was an old log building left over from Russian days, and after it burned to the ground Dr. Jackson led the crew that salvaged the lumber from an abandoned salmon cannery and constructed the first building on the present campus.

Congress at first declined to appropriate funds to buy reindeer in Siberia, but Dr. Jackson raised enough money himself to start the program and to prove that the animals could safely be transported across the Bering Sea to Alaska.

Alice Postell in *Where Did the Reindeer Come From?* tells the fascinating story of Dr. Jackson's reindeer endeavor and subsequent events, one of the great epics of the North.

R. N. DeArmond

Acknowledgments

The interest and support of family and many friends have been invaluable in completing this book. A partial list includes a number of people on the campus of Sheldon Jackson College in Sitka, Alaska: Peter Corey, Curator and Director of Sheldon Jackson Museum and Evelyn Bonner, Librarian, and Nancy Ricketts, Archivist, at Stratton Library on the campus. I would also like to thank Robert DeArmond, one of Alaska's leading historians; Dr. Robert A. Dieterich, Institute of Arctic Biology, University of Alaska, Fairbanks; Senator Ted Stevens, who guided my first visit to the National Archives; Reverend John and Barbara Shaffer; Norma Hoyt; Gary Holthaus; and Zelma Doig. My editor, Susan Page York, and book designer John Laursen have been extra helpful in their professions.

Preface

March 1983

March is still full-blown winter in the remote village of Shishmaref on an island spit hugging the coastline of the Chukchi Sea, Seward Peninsula, Alaska. Ice binds the area into one solid whole with the mainland, and extends as far as the eye reaches to seaward.

The elementary and high school, plus the church, have brought to this village of some 500 Eskimos the only outsiders. Their subsistence living is augmented with works of art from walrus ivory, reindeer antler, and from the most recently discovered medium, whalebone. Periodically a dealer will come from the urban centers and buy all the handiwork that has been stockpiled. It is a rare privilege for an individual to purchase some of this art directly from the artist, and to feel that the local artist might benefit, without the complexities of the various middleman enterprises.

A herd of reindeer was being driven into a corral near Shishmaref for the purpose of separating the nucleus of a new herd. I had been invited to watch the work, but a blizzard had delayed the arrival of the herd. Furthermore, the windchill of minus eighty made the three-mile ride on a snowmobile very unattractive to my three-score years and ten!

Elsie Weyiouanna was sitting on the floor, the furry skin from the leg of a reindeer lying on a short piece of board between her legs. Following traditional methods of tanning, she was scraping the inside clean of fat and flesh, preparing to make knee-high mukluks for a member of her family. Her husband Alex was hammering on a plywood partition. He was patiently making slow progress in finishing the "modern" home for his family while they continued their daily activities all around him. Meanwhile, heavy parkas and mukluks were left along the wall as various members of three generations stopped in for hot coffee and conversation.

While we awaited the arrival of the herd, we sang the old hymns so dear to the hearts of all of us, as I accompanied with music on a well-preserved old-fashioned organ. Warm hospitality proved most conducive to visiting.

When Elsie Weyiouanna asked "Where did the first reindeer come from, and when?" it seemed to me I had heard the question so many times that it was time to write a comprehensive story of the origins of the domestic reindeer in Alaska. So began this book.

Introduction

The way of life of Alaskan Eskimos changed dramatically when white men came to Alaska, beginning in the last half of the eighteenth century. Then, in the last decade of the nineteenth century, came prospects of the means for Eskimos to enter the white man's economic pattern of life, while retaining self-respect and part of their culture—a culture adapted to the rigors of Arctic life. That prospect is the foundation of the story of domestic reindeer. The story of the first fifty years of the reindeer industry is an important part of Alaska's history, deserving of more comprehensive coverage than it has received.

My aim is to tell of the reindeer industry in northwestern and northern Alaska, from the original idea for introducing domestic reindeer brought to the attention of the U.S. government in 1890, to the roundup of all non-Native owned herds in the winter of 1939-1940 following the Reindeer Act of 1937, which limited reindeer ownership to Native Alaskans. This story extends westward to Siberia, far southeastward to the capital of the United States, and across the Atlantic to northern Europe.

The story unfolds within a larger story of Eskimos in transition from their traditional culture. It encompasses the efforts of government officials, missionaries, and others who believed that aid could and should be provided to the peoples of Alaska; the Lapps who came to tend the first reindeer and teach reindeer husbandry; and the Eskimos who took up reindeer herding.

Certain events loom large in the introduction of domestic reindeer into Alaska. One event is the expedition to help stranded whalers at Point Barrow. Reindeer also figured in the intended relief of miners on the Yukon. Some of the events described show the rigorous Alaskan life before modernization. They also illustrate the attitudes of "outsiders"—from missionaries to gold miners, teachers to traders.

The cast of characters in the story of the reindeer is large. I describe the outsiders who appear to have played the most prominent roles in the reindeer industry during the period 1890-1940. Also described are individual Eskimos whose lives represent the spirit of a courageous and hospitable people, a people caught up in and tossed by the tides of change which came to the land that is their home. The stories of these individuals are known mostly as they told them to others. First person accounts of Eskimos are difficult to come by because of the lack of a written Eskimo language.

The story related here was developed from a number of sources. I drew information about the establishment and management of the first herds from the annual *Report on Introduction of Domestic Reindeer into Alaska*, which was submitted for each fiscal year (July-June). Sheldon Jackson's annual *Reports* to Congress for the U.S. Department of the Interior cover the years from 1891 through 1905. The final *Report*, not published until 1908, includes accounts written by white inhabitants of Alaska in response to an unfavorable 1905 report by Frank Churchill, who was sent by the federal government to report on the handling of the reindeer project.

Daily journals from the various reindeer stations, which appeared as appendices to Jackson's *Reports*, are a rich source of information. They record such details as weather conditions, handling of reindeer, chores of herders and other personnel, housing conditions, problems of health, and personality conflicts. These writings by people who were there give us a picture of what daily life was like along the Bering Sea and in Arctic Alaska during the first fifteen years of the reindeer industry.

Carl Lomen's *Fifty Years in Alaska* provides a useful review of the years from 1900 to 1950, from the viewpoint of a businessman. Clarence L. Andrews' books on Eskimo life cover the seven years (1923-1929) that he spent among them as a teacher. During the most controversial years he wrote numerous newspaper articles and letters defending the Eskimos' point of view.

A study by the Arctic biology department at the University of Alaska, Fairbanks, gives an overview of the reindeer industry from the beginning until now. Information was also obtained in personal interviews conducted on the Seward Peninsula and from oral history tapes in the archives of the Kegoayah Kozga Library at Nome. The Bibliography includes other publications about the reindeer industry, Eskimo life, and outsiders who became involved.

The written records researched in Alaska were at the Stratton Library of Sheldon Jackson College in Sitka; the Elmer E. Rasmussen Library at the University of Alaska in Fairbanks; and the Alaska State Historical Library in Juneau. Other historical records were reviewed at the University of Washington, Seattle; at the University of Oregon, Eugene, in the C. L. Andrews Collection; and in the National Archives, Washington, D.C.

Intending no disrespect, I have used terms as they appeared in writings of the time, for the sake of historical accuracy. For example, the word "native" appears in this story, rather than "Native." During most of the time period covered, Native Alaskans were referred to as natives. Only after legislation in the late 1930s did the word "Native" appear. The Sami who came to Alaska from northern Europe are called Lapps, as they were by the people of the time.

Because they vary in different reports and books, I have had to decide how to spell certain names. Spellings for Eskimo and Russian personal and place names are standardized. Without a dictionary for Eskimo names and no Russian dictionary at hand, different writers down through the years used different spellings of the same proper names. For example, the village spelled "Sinruk" here has at various times down through the years been spelled Sinuk, Sinrook, or Sinrock.

Distances and other numbers given are those that appear in reports. Exactness was impossible. Distances were difficult to measure. In connection with reindeer, numbers vary considerably in the different accounts of the time. This variation is perhaps in part because counts of the herds were made at different times of the year. Inconsistency in reindeer counts from one year to another is probably partly accounted for by losses due to predation, sickness, use for food, and rustling. Rustling of deer was a problem just as cattle rustling was in the States. Reindeer also sometimes followed their cousins, the wild caribou.

The photographs are from a number of sources. All of the libraries previously mentioned have separate files of photographs.

The Glenbow Archives of Calgary, Canada, provided their catalog of over sixty large albums of original photographs taken by the Lomen brothers. Many were selected to illustrate this book.

Although the story of Eskimos and reindeer is a continuing one, I stopped at 1940. But when there is conversation about domestic reindeer in Alaska, the question is usually asked, "What is happening to them now, and what does the future look like?" To obtain an answer I contacted Dr. Robert Dieterich of the Institute of Arctic Biology at the University of Alaska, Fairbanks. Based on conversations with him, I have added an Epilogue which gives a snapshot view of the reindeer industry today.

It seems to me that the domestic reindeer offer Alaskan Eskimos an opportunity to have an assured comfortable subsistence when nature develops those unpredictable extra-lean years. The coastal villages that depend on walrus and/or whale for their winter diet could have reindeer herds in reserve, to be rounded up and brought in when needed. Young people should be able to raise a few animals, much in the pattern of Future Farmers of America, finding satisfaction and pride in ownership.

The reindeer reproduce quickly. There is a ready market for reindeer meat in Alaska, one that appears to be growing in part because the meat does not carry the high cost of shipping from the Lower 48.

A high commendation for the raising of reindeer is that they are compatible with the environment. Furthermore, reindeer are a renewable resource.

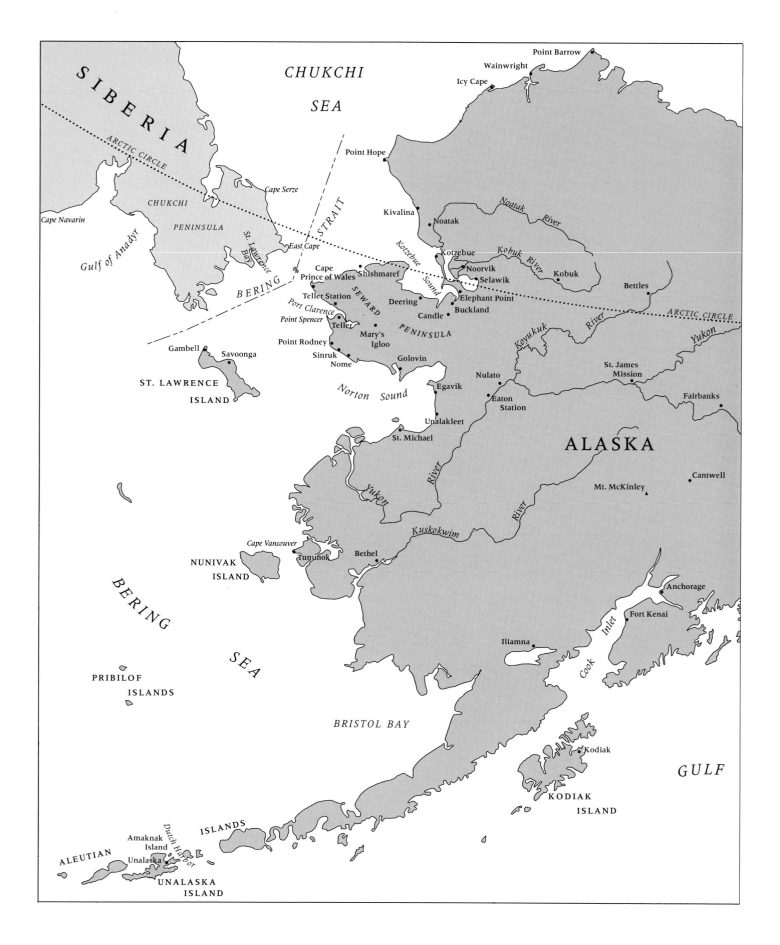

SIBERIA

CHUKCHI SEA

ARCTIC CIRCLE

Cape Serze

CHUKCHI PENINSULA

Cape Navarin

Gulf of Anadyr

St. Lawrence Bay

East Cape

BERING

STRAIT

Point Hope

Point Barrow

Wainwright

Icy Cape

Kivalina

Noatak

Noatak River

Kotzebue

Kobuk River

Noorvik

Selawik

Kobuk

Bettles

Cape Prince of Wales

Shishmaref

Kotzebue Sound

Elephant Point

Deering

Buckland

ARCTIC CIRCLE

Teller Station

SEWARD

Candle

River

Yukon

Port Clarence

Point Spencer

Teller

Mary's Igloo

PENINSULA

Koyukuk

Gambell

Savoonga

Point Rodney

Sinruk

Nome

Golovin

St. James Mission

ST. LAWRENCE ISLAND

Egavik

Nulato

Fairbanks

Norton Sound

Eaton Station

ALASKA

Unalakleet

St. Michael

Cantwell

Mt. McKinley

Yukon

River

BERING

Kuskokwim

Cape Vancouver

Tununok

Bethel

NUNIVAK ISLAND

SEA

Anchorage

Fort Kenai

Iliamna

PRIBILOF ISLANDS

Cook Inlet

BRISTOL BAY

Kodiak

GULF

KODIAK ISLAND

ISLANDS

Amaknak Island

Dutch Harbor

ALEUTIAN

Unalaska

UNALASKA ISLAND

xxii

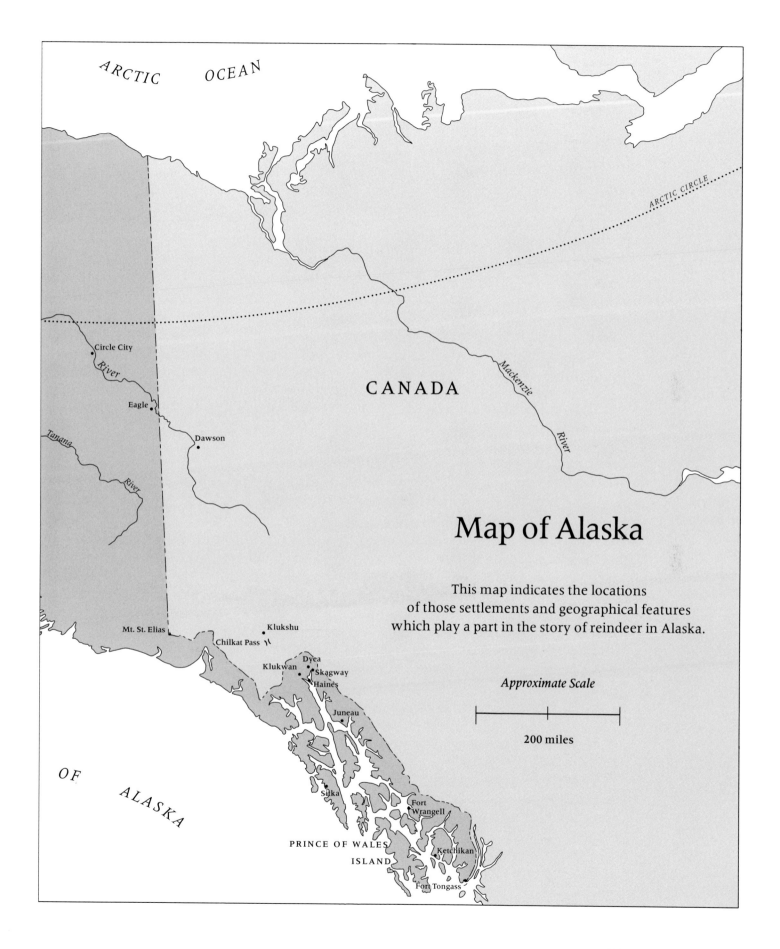

ARCTIC   OCEAN

CANADA

Circle City

Eagle

Dawson

Tanana

River

River

Mackenzie

River

Map of Alaska

This map indicates the locations
of those settlements and geographical features
which play a part in the story of reindeer in Alaska.

Mt. St. Elias

Chilkat Pass

Klukshu

Klukwan

Dyea

Skagway

Haines

Juneau

Approximate Scale

├────────┼────────┤

200 miles

O F

A L A S K A

Sitka

Fort
Wrangell

PRINCE OF WALES

ISLAND

Ketchikan

Fort Tongass

ARCTIC CIRCLE

Where Did the Reindeer Come From?

1

Early Alaska and the Ipani

Alaska's geography and vastness are difficult to grasp without exploring the region. The people who live in Alaska today and have coped with the extremities of its climate remain in awe of the earliest residents who adapted their way of life to the environment.

The Place

With the mountain ranges and rivers establishing their own variations of climate, the peoples of Alaska once survived mostly from season to season as hunters and gatherers. The Alaskan Indians were established in the interior, mainly south and east of the Yukon River, while the Eskimos and Aleuts inhabited the coastal areas, the Aleutian Islands, St. Lawrence Island, and other islands in the Bering Sea. The history related in this book focuses on the Eskimos of northwestern and northern Alaska.

The Yukon River and its hundreds of miles of tributaries were once the lifeline for all who lived along their banks. A major North American river, the Yukon empties into the Bering Sea at the southern end of Norton Sound, dividing Alaska into two almost equal areas.

Navigable for some 2,000 miles during the brief northland summer, the Yukon is a raging torrent during the spring. Runoffs break up the heavy ice that gradually builds up to gigantic battering rams along the Yukon's banks. Tearing away earth and trees—and everything else in its way—this force continues to build the delta where river meets sea and deposits an abundant supply of logs. These logs float along the coast, becoming building material and firewood for Eskimos along the northern coast—where no trees grow.

The Ipani Way of Life

Through the generations, Eskimos learned how best to survive in the harsh environment of the subarctic and arctic region they call home. A subsistence life style with an abundance of sea mammals, fish, and land game provided adequate food, clothing, and shelter for the Ipani, or "long-time-ago Eskimos."

Subsistence depended upon wildlife that was seasonal, and success in securing food was carefully taught from one generation to the next. Women learned food preparation at an early age. They also learned how to make the skin clothing and footwear so crucial to survival.

Among the Arctic whale hunters, the great whales were the prime food source. However, if none was killed in a particular

Whales

From time immemorial Eskimos have hunted whales for a large source of protein and oil so vital to survival in their frigid world. The small white beluga, 12 to 15 feet long, become a choice feast when they approach the coastline to feed or to have their young.

A village hunts the big baleen whales in order to lay up their needs for the long winter. The oil, as much as 150 barrels from one whale, can be used not only for food, but can be burned for heat or light, used in soapmaking, and used as a mechanical lubricant.

Of ten species of baleen whales the most commonly known are the bowhead, humpback, gray, and right whale. The largest of all, the blue whale, can be 100 feet in length and weigh an average of one ton per foot.

The baleen are multiple bony overlapping strips suspended from the upper jawbone of the whale. The largest whales reportedly have as many as 400 strips on each side of their upper jaw, graduating in length up to twelve feet. On the average, each strip is six to eight inches wide tapering to a feathered point as it curls under the huge tongue. The edges next to the tongue are fringed, thus forming a sieve for retaining the plankton and small seafood that the whale is constantly foraging for in the ocean waters.

Before spring steel was developed at the turn of the century, the tough, flexible baleen strips were manufactured commercially into skirt hoops, corset stays, buggywhips, and various kinds of spring suspensions.

A popular—but very expensive—tourist item of recent years is the baleen basket. Around 1913 the trader, Charles Brower, brought some weavers of willow baskets from farther south to teach the Point Barrow Eskimos. Using fine strips of baleen, various sizes of beautiful black or brown baskets are made, often decorated with ivory carvings on the cover.

The baleen whales were hunted nearly to extinction in the 1800s. Whaling ships from Great Britain and the New England states sought their harvest in spite of Arctic storms and frozen seas. Many ships were lost each year as storms caught them in the ice.

Between 1871 and 1888 some 70 whaleships were wrecked in the Arctic Ocean. Over 400 men were rescued from freezing or starving to death by the U.S. Revenue Marine cutters. William Bixby's book *Track of the Bear* gives a fascinating account of the cutter *Bear*.

While the Eskimos witnessed commercial whaling, they continued in their customary use of this rich resource. One or two whales would provide a village with a year's supply of meat as well as oil and baleen for many uses. To this day, the Eskimos need their quota of whales in order to survive the long, cold, dark winter. Only Native Alaskans are allowed to kill sea mammals under the Sea Mammals Act of 1971.

year, seals, walrus, and beluga whales offered an alternative for survival. Eskimos on the Bering Sea coast had the same choices.

By contrast, the life of the caribou hunters of the interior was very hard in the years when the caribou herds did not show up in the expected areas. Only good runs of salmon were an adequate alternative as the primary source of nourishment. Other fish, such as pike, turbot, and trout, were simply not worth the effort to gather in quantities for storage.

Watching for the hibernation den of a bear and skillfully probing for the animal for winter food was no task for an amateur. Animals that were trapped became both meat and clothing. Young boys were included on hunting trips—to learn survival in all kinds of weather and emergencies. The big moment in a boy's life was his first kill, which was usually a smaller animal, such as a seal. An important ceremony would then proclaim him a "man."

June was the busiest time of the year above the Arctic Circle. Because the sun never goes down during this month, work could go on as long as the Ipani were willing. By contrast, December saw the least activity. During this month it is as dark at noon as it is at midnight, and extremely cold—as much as 50 or 60 below zero.

Gathering eggs of the seagulls, ducks, and geese was an important part of subsistence living. During the nesting seasons of these migratory birds, thousands of eggs were gathered. But always enough were left in the nest for another season's generation.

With sacks on their backs the men would wade the shallow, just-thawed lakes and ponds, to locate the nests. Using moss to protect the eggs, they soon filled their packsacks. Hungry after their work, they might build a fire and steam some eggs wrapped in wet moss. When cooked the eggs were put

Hunting Ducks with Native Sling   (Eskimo Drawing)

Courtesy of National Archives.

Carrying the caribou home. Native drawing in the 1894 *Report on Introduction of Domestic Reindeer into Alaska.*

into cold water, peeled, and eaten. Another method for cooking eggs was to cut a green willow branch as big around as the egg. After hammering the bark lightly, the stem was removed and the egg closed inside the bark for steaming.

June was also the time for hunting seal and for hunting beluga, the white, twelve- to fourteen-foot whale that was (and still is) such an abundant and important source of food. As the ice thawed away from the shore, belugas would come in to feed or to have their young. Hunters in as many as 15 to 20 sealskin kayaks would close in on the feeding belugas and drive them into shallow water where each Eskimo would catch two or three and kill them with a spear.

The most common way of storing food for winter was in seal-pokes. An Eskimo woman would remove the seal skin entirely, beginning from the mouth. After scraping off all the fat and meat she would blow the skin up so it looked like a big balloon, then close it tightly while it dried. The skin then was ready to be filled with oil from the seal or the whale. Each family also would use many seal-pokes for storing dried fish, spring greens, and dried meat of the seal and walrus, usually preserving the food in oil.

If a family had more than needed, the extra oil was used in trade for caribou skins and other resources from inland areas. Oil was used in trade with Siberian deermen as well.

2

Tides of Change

Historical records show Russian explorers reached the remote northern shores of North America as early as the mid-1700s. Among the first were Vitus Bering and Aleksei Chirikov in their two ships, the *St. Peter* and *St. Paul*. In 1741 Bering sighted Mt. St. Elias. Chirikov reached what is now Prince of Wales Island.

Early Outsiders

Soon, beautiful sea otter skins were carried back to St. Petersburg. This caused a rush of hunters and traders who crowded the waters along the Aleutian Chain and the southern coastline of what is now Alaska.

By 1763, Catherine II had assigned naval officers to the vessels of the fur hunters to keep ship journals and to assure proper treatment of the native people. In 1794 a Russian Orthodox religious mission began work with the Kodiak and Aleut peoples. From this beginning contact with the outside world, those people who already were living in the northland had to accommodate to changes in their way of life.

Russia didn't claim the territory that Bering and Chirikov had "discovered" until 1824. In an agreement with the United States and Great Britain, the southern coast of present day Alaska became the southern limit of Russian America. In 1867 Russian America was sold to the United States.

At the time of purchase, the U.S. War Department sent troops to Fort Tongass, Fort Wrangell, Sitka, Fort Kenai, Kodiak, and the Pribilof Islands. These troups were a controlling force within the limited areas they were able to oversee. Except for this presence, the government gave little attention to what was happening in Alaska.

Whaling ships continued to pull fortunes from the Arctic waters as they stripped oil and baleen from bowhead whales. Others killed walrus for the money they could make from walrus tusks. Hunters with the new breech-loading guns killed off—and drove off—the caribou. Seemingly few if any outsiders who hunted gave a thought to the effect on the subsistence living of Eskimos.

The fur seal also was a source of income, primarily for outsiders. Policing of the Seal Islands (Pribilofs) was one of the priority assignments of the Revenue Marine Service. Poaching and illegal pelagic, or open sea, killing of the females for their much prized fur almost exterminated the rookeries. (Estimated at 4,500,000 in 1867, the seal population dwindled to 215,000 by 1912. Not until 1911 was an International Fur Seal Convention establishing international quotas signed by the United States, Great Britain, Russia, and Japan.)

Traders did a thriving business in the carvings and furs that the people of the north had. However, the Eskimos had little or no experience with the value of goods offered to them in trade compared to the value of their own trade items. It was all too easy at first to cheat them of what would be considered a fair return in the white economy.

Rum-runners, whalers, and others offered alcohol to anyone who would buy or trade. Problems associated with drinking were common. Particularly devastating, however, was the effect on the independence of those Eskimos who took up drinking: they no longer carried on their usual activities to make their living and so became dependent on their families or whites.

The Revenue Marine Service (at times called the Revenue Cutter Service) first sent a cutter to patrol the waters of the Bering Sea and Arctic Ocean in 1867. Michael A. Healy, who would become a major early figure in the start-up of the reindeer industry, first came to the Bering Sea in 1869 on the cutter *Reliance*. He was then a lieutenant.

The men aboard the cutters provided the only semblance of law and order in Alaskan waters. Their duties included search and rescue, protecting seals and arresting poachers, transporting government officials, towing whalers to port, providing food to Eskimos, and collecting customs. The men also provided medical service to both whites and nonwhites during the few months that the sea was not solid with ice.

In 1877 the last of the troops were withdrawn from the small colony at Sitka and sent to protect citizens in Idaho against threatened Indian attacks. Sergeant J. S. Brown sent a letter to the YMCA in Portland, Oregon, before he left Fort Wrangell. Brown sent a second letter to General Howard, who commanded the Military Department of the Columbia at Portland. Each letter pleaded for someone to come and help the Indians living around the fort. His letters explained how the Alaskan Indians had learned a little about Christianity and wanted to learn more. He was also concerned about the influence of the miners and traders, and the problems caused by liquor traffic.

A copy of one of Sergeant Brown's letters reached Reverend Sheldon Jackson at the General Assembly of the Presbyterian church gathered in Chicago in May 1877. Deeply moved by what he read, Reverend Jackson sent the letter to be published in the

Dr. Sheldon Jackson, General Agent of Education in Alaska from 1885 to 1906. Born in Minaville, New York in 1834, Jackson graduated from Union College in 1855. Two years later he graduated from Princeton Seminary and was ordained by the Presbytery of Albany. His first trip to Alaska was in 1877. Photograph by LaRoche, Seattle, Washington, 1899. Courtesy of National Archives.

Chicago Daily Tribune. Very soon thereafter he also had it published in the leading papers of the Presbyterian church throughout the United States.

The very first Presbyterian missionary to Alaska was Mrs. Amanda McFarland, the widow of one of Jackson's minister friends. She was ready and eager to go, but her friends would not let her go alone. So this was Jackson's "call" in 1877 to go to Alaska.

He sent a letter to his wife, and took the next steamer for Alaska as escort for Mrs. McFarland. Arriving at Fort Wrangell, Jackson located a log carpenter shop where Mrs. McFarland organized her classroom with 27 books that she had brought with her.

Jackson then made an exploratory trip along the coast, only to learn that all the troops had been recalled home. There would be no government officer to enforce any kind of law and order in all of Alaska. After returning to check on the new school, Jackson went straight to the U.S. capital, where he began his lifelong dedication to the welfare of the native peoples of Alaska.

Starting Government Schools

In 1884 the U.S. Congress passed the Harrison Act, creating a form of government for Alaska, appropriating funds for schools, and establishing a General Agent of Education with an office in the nation's capital. The

Dr. Sheldon Jackson, Mr. William T. Lopp, Mr. Bruce Gibson, and (unidentified) others at the school house, Cape Prince of Wales, 1892. Courtesy of Department of History, Presbyterian Church, U.S.A.

Eskimo Art

For some 2,000 years, Eskimos engraved ivory with silhouettes of their activities, such as harpooning whale, taking caribou with bow and arrow, driving dog sleds, wrestling, foot racing, and dancing. The ivory usually was in the form of long, narrow handles for bow drills or for tool bags.

In the 1890s, teachers in the newly formed government and mission schools supplied Eskimos with paper, pencils, ink, crayons, and water colors —materials unseen before in northwestern Alaska. With these new art materials, Eskimos continued to represent their activities as well as scenes from the land. Most of the sketches surviving from about 1890 to 1900 are drawn on the unlined side of school tablet paper, probably because of the scarcity of paper in some of the Bureau of Education schools.

Many of the sketches that still exist show much detail and familiarity with Eskimo activities. This suggests the artists were approaching or in early adulthood, not young school children. Their drawings (some of which appear in the Phebus book listed in the Bibliography) provide a record of Alaskan Eskimo life from the Eskimo artists' viewpoint, and before the dramatic changes that came in the twentieth century.

agent was expected to travel in the District of Alaska during most of the year and establish schools.

In 1885, Sheldon Jackson was appointed Alaska's first General Agent of Education by U.S. Secretary of the Interior Henry M. Teller. Jackson had at his disposal $25,000 to establish government schools over a two-year period in a territory one-fifth the size of today's contiguous United States. Not a single schoolhouse had yet been provided for a population of more than 33,400 people, more than 30,000 of whom were Eskimos, Aleuts, and Indians who had not seen the inside of a schoolroom except where there were mission schools. There were about 7,000 children of school age.

The work of establishing schools began first in southeastern Alaska, referred to as the Panhandle. Most of the white settlers were in this area, where the climatic conditions were more favorable than in the northwestern and Arctic coastal areas. Once work was underway in the Panhandle, Jackson turned his attention northward, to education for the Eskimos. Because of the difficulty of obtaining adequate building materials and of transporting those materials, a number of schools were begun through contracts with church missions that already had usable buildings.

3

The Reindeer Project is Born

Sheldon Jackson gave much consideration to what kind of schools would be best in northern Alaska. He knew it was important to take into account the living circumstances of Eskimos, which were very different from those of Indians in southern Alaska, both in food supply and physical setting.

The depletion of Eskimo food sources was an important concern of Jackson's, one shared by others from the United States who had knowledge of the Eskimo way of life and felt a responsibility toward the people who had lived in northern Alaska before white men arrived. Another concern was how to help the Eskimos adapt to the white man's economy, for it was clear that white men had come to stay.

An Idea Leads to Action

As early as 1885, Charles H. Townsend, a zoologist working with the U.S. Fish Commission, wrote in a report to Congress about the idea of bringing domestic reindeer to Alaska. He noted that there were large herds of domestic reindeer kept by the Chukchis on the Asiatic side of Bering Strait and that people on both sides of the strait communicated regularly.

In 1890, Jackson went on the annual cruise of the revenue cutter *Bear*. By this time, Michael Healy had been captain of the *Bear* for four years.

After visiting villages in the Bering Sea area, Jackson wrote a preliminary report to the U.S. Commissioner of Education on the introduction of reindeer into Alaska. The report stated that the reindeer could be a source of food, clothing, transportation, and employment, and that Eskimos could readily adapt from hunting, which could no longer be a mainstay, to reindeer herding, whose benefits they would readily see. (Characteristics of domestic reindeer are described in Appendix A, beginning on page 90.)

Captain Healy also saw potential benefits in bringing domestic reindeer from Siberia to the Bering Sea coast of Alaska. Healy was well acquainted with the people on both sides of the Sea, for he had been cruising the waters and stopping along both coasts for twenty years. He knew the problems of survival during the long winter in northwestern and northern Alaska, and the extremities of the climate in which the Eskimos lived.

Healy added his voice in support of a reindeer project. He wrote to the Commissioner of Education, describing the living conditions which he had observed among the Eskimos.

In his letter, Healy proposed that domestic reindeer be considered as tools for training young Eskimo men, much the same as the

Bureau of Education was establishing industrial schools among Indian boys in the states, providing animals and equipment to teach them to raise stock. In Healy's view, introduction of tame reindeer into Alaska for the Eskimos would be a humanitarian activity that would do more to make their lives better than any standard schools or charities.

Overcoming Early Challenges

And so the reindeer project was born. Sheldon Jackson would oversee the project for the U.S. government. The U.S. Secretary of State secured instructions from the Russian government to their officers on the Siberian coast to support the sale of reindeer. Captain Healy was instructed to assist in any way he could. Healy's endorsement of the reindeer enterprise proved to be invaluable to Jackson.

With the first step taken to bring domestic reindeer to Alaska, challenges still remained. Records of the earliest years of the reindeer industry reveal many difficulties.

Communication was not easy between Washington, the U.S. capital, where Sheldon Jackson maintained an office, and Alaska. Messages, relayed by various means, were sometimes delayed or inaccurate.

If Jackson was in Washington, the people who were responsible for carrying out the day-to-day work with the Eskimos had to make decisions without consulting him. And when Jackson was in Alaska, he could not be in daily or even weekly contact with the Department of the Interior and certainly could not receive any immediate instructions from the Secretary.

Another difficulty was the lack of federal funding for the reindeer project. While Congress approved the idea of the reindeer industry effort, it did not set aside any monies. Not until 1894 would federal financial support become available.

Captain Michael A. Healy, U.S. Revenue Marine, Commander of the *Bear*, 1892. Courtesy of Department of History, Presbyterian Church, U.S.A.

Jackson did not wait. Instead, with the approval of the Commissioner of Education, he wrote articles for a number of newspapers in the eastern United States and leading church publications. He described the conditions he found among the Eskimos and set forth his proposal to start a domestic reindeer industry for their benefit with deer from Siberia. These articles met with much sympathy among readers, who responded generously to help pay for bringing the first reindeer to Alaska.

Even with funds available, Jackson faced another obstacle. The Secretary of State had secured instructions from the Russian government to its officers on the Siberian coast to support the sale of reindeer, but Jackson had to get the reindeer herders of Siberia—the Chukchis—to sell live reindeer to him.

The Siberian herders gained their livelihood in part by bartering reindeer products for goods that came from across the sea. For as far back as anyone could remember it was the custom to barter for seal oil from Alaskan Eskimos in exchange for reindeer skins. What of trading live deer? The Siberians' fathers never had done this.

If herds were established across the sea might that not ruin their business with the

---

Michael Healy

Michael Healy was one of ten children born to Michael Morris Healy, a plantation owner not far from Macon, Georgia, and his mulatto slave Elisa Smith. Elisa lived with Healy as his wife. The children were kept on the plantation until about the age of ten. The elder Healy knew that they would be considered slaves in case of his death, so he sent them north, one at a time, to be well educated in the best Quaker and Catholic boarding schools.

Michael was born in 1839. He lost his parents when he was only eleven. Within the next four years he had run away from three schools—in Massachusetts, Montreal, and Paris. At 16 he was on the seas as a cabin boy. He was an officer on a merchant vessel by age 24.

In 1868 Healy made his first cruise to Alaska with the U.S. Revenue Marine Service, and by 1883 was a full captain, in charge of the cutter *Corwin*. A Congressional citation in 1885 praised officers and crew for their "heroic deeds" in Alaskan waters. The citation pointed out the extensive 20,000 mile coastline, twice that of all other U.S. coastline, for which Congress provided one revenue ship.

One year after the citation Healy received a larger ship, the *Bear*. He continued to teach the harsh discipline needed to cope with the wind, fog, and ice, and to deal with the illegal trafficking in liquor and fur-seal skins. While Healy was not well liked by young officers who resented his harsh seaman's discipline, he was well-known in Arctic waters as rescuer, protector, judge, and administrator of justice.

In 1895 Healy was making his twenty-second annual cruise with a young ship's doctor aboard who did not know the North, and a sulky batch of new officers. By the time the *Bear*, captain, and crew returned to San Francisco, tempers had erupted, along with Healy's drinking, and the young officers requested a court-martial to investigate Healy's drinking behavior. This ended in a hearing that suspended Healy from service for four years and had him publicly reprimanded.

The Nome Gold Rush brought new demands on the Revenue Marine Service. When another Revenue captain died unexpectedly in 1900, Healy was given command of the new cutter *McCullock*. But on returning from Nome to Unalaska on that cruise, Healy got word that he was to be transferred to a small cutter in Boston Harbor. It meant demotion to where he was 25 years earlier. Quick-thinking officers and crew kept him from jumping overboard. During the night he managed to slash his wrist with the crystal of a watch.

Admirers of Healy among whalers and others of the North rallied to his support while he was hospitalized in San Francisco. They petitioned the new Secretary of the Treasury, Lyman Gage, to reinstate the Captain.

Healy's case was reviewed by the new federal administration in 1902. Superiors decided he had been dealt with too harshly. He was restored to his original rank, and given command of the *Thetis*. He continued as captain for two more years, until retirement at age 65.

A year after retirement he died. In San Francisco he was honored with flags at half-mast, and officers of the Revenue Service attended his funeral in gold braid. His coffin was carried by crewmen of the *Bear*.

Eskimos? What if a man should sell his deer and the following winter should bring illness or calamity of any kind to his herd or his family? The Shaman would blame it all on the sale of those live deer.

Still, Jackson and Healy were determined to purchase reindeer. Jackson exchanged the money he had received in donations from supporters of the reindeer project for barter goods that Healy recommended based on his knowledge from previous trav-els among the people of the Siberian coast.

In the spring of 1891, with the barter goods on board the *Bear*, Jackson and Healy proceeded to those coastal areas of Siberia where Healy knew that the reindeer were concentrated.

Upon his arrival, Jackson found that the Siberian herders were suspicious of his designs. They had dealt with other white men who had failed to keep their promises. They could not understand what was wanted with

Built in 1874 at Dundee, Newfoundland, the *Bear* was sent on a rescue expedition into the Arctic in 1884. In 1885 the ship was transferred from the U.S. Navy to the Treasury Department Revenue Marine Service, Bering Sea Patrol, where it served for 41 years. Courtesy of National Archives.

On September 21, 1891, the first small group of reindeer landed on Amaknak Island, Alaska, proving that the deer could be transported alive from Siberia. Photograph in the 1894 *Report on Introduction of Domestic Reindeer into Alaska*.

the reindeer: the idea of helping others without pay was foreign. However, the herders knew Captain Healy. His official capacity and the presence of the revenue cutter gave Jackson a degree of respect and trust among these deermen, easing his contact.

First Reindeer Purchase

When Jackson left on the first voyage to purchase reindeer, he knew that newspaper reports in the United States had stimulated widespread general interest in the reindeer project, and there had already been much public discussion. The critics said the deer would not survive being transported across the Bering Sea, or the dogs among the Eskimos would kill the deer, or Eskimos would kill the deer for food.

Jackson realized the need for caution and diplomatic wisdom, not only because of the Siberians' unease, but also because of criticism at home. In 1891 he purchased only

16 deer. These were hoisted onto the *Bear*, which then sailed over 1,500 miles along the Siberian coast, calling at various villages where Healy and Jackson held conferences with the leading reindeer owners. On this trip arrangements were made for the purchase of animals the following season.

The first reindeer were landed in good condition on Amaknak Island in the harbor of Unalaska. They had survived three weeks aboard ship, much of the time on a very stormy sea. Sheldon Jackson had proven that reindeer could be purchased from the Siberian deermen—alive. And he had proved that they could be transported by ship from Siberia to Alaska.

When he arrived in Unalaska on May 22 of the following year, Jackson found that all but two of the reindeer left the preceding fall on Amaknak had wintered successfully and were in good condition. Two deer had fallen to their death with the collapse of an overhanging snowdrift. Happily, two reindeer calves had been born.

4

An Industry Gets Under Way

The transfer of domestic reindeer onto the American continent began in 1892. Sheldon Jackson and Michael Healy once again set out for Siberia aboard the *Bear*. They arrived off Cape Navarin on June 6 and proceeded up the coast. Progress was slow in the heavy fields of ice, in spite of the strong ice-breaking construction of the *Bear*. Two anchors were lost and one of the propeller blades was broken on this difficult journey.

Hoisting reindeer onto the *Bear*. Courtesy of National Archives.

Undaunted, Healy and his crew continued until they had made five trips to Siberia. A total of 171 deer were landed between July 4 and August 10 at Port Clarence, on the central western coast of Seward Peninsula. Four Siberian herders, who had agreed to care for the herd and begin training young Eskimos to reindeer herding, were also brought over.

Teller Reindeer Station

For the first reindeer station, Jackson selected an area that would provide a good supply of reindeer moss and fresh water for the animals. He chose a location at Port Clarence which had been previously used as a watering station by the whalers because it was readily approachable most of the time, had good anchorage, and was only about 40 or 50 miles from the Bering Strait.

In fact, Jackson had reported on his first visit in July of 1890 that there were 25 whalers at anchor off Point Spencer, which lies within Port Clarence. These whalers were awaiting the arrival of the annual supply ship from San Francisco. On its voyage back to San Francisco the supply ship would carry the whalers' spring catch of baleen.

The place where the ships anchored had been marked by the whalers with a driftwood log high on the beach, topped by an

Landing the first reindeer at Teller Station, July 4, 1892. Courtesy of Department of History, Presbyterian Church, U.S.A.

empty barrel. On July 4, 1892, when the first 53 domestic reindeer bounded across the tundra beyond this shoreline, Jackson hoisted a United States flag atop the log.

A few days later lumber and building materials were unloaded from the *Bear*. Captain Healy sent his carpenters and crew members ashore to erect a frame house 20 by 60 feet in size. However, the building was not completed before the Arctic winter set in. The newly named reindeer superintendent, Mr. Miner W. Bruce of Nebraska, constructed a dugout for himself and his assistant, Bruce Gibson of California, and another for the four Siberian herders.

In a report to Jackson, Bruce wrote about work—serious and not so serious— with the reindeer. (Bruce's account of breaking reindeer to harness and a reindeer sleigh ride appears as Appendix B, beginning on page 92.)

This first reindeer station was named Teller Station in honor of Congressman Henry M. Teller who, when he was the Secretary of the Interior, had appointed Jackson to be the first Agent of Education in Alaska, and who was an ardent supporter of the reindeer project.

Schools and Herding Apprenticeships

Along the Bering Sea coast of Alaska there were no white settlers at the time, except at the ports of Unalaska and St. Michael. However, there were 19 mission stations in the areas where most Eskimos made their homes: 3 on the Arctic Ocean, 9 on the Bering Sea, 7 in the valley of the Yukon River —with a total of 61 missionaries. It was natural to combine standard education and the reindeer project.

Jackson outlined policies for the distribution and management of reindeer, as well as for the apprenticeships of Eskimos. His goal was to establish and build herds as quickly as possible.

Herding required a form of discipline and rewards that were different from those essential to hunting. Jackson was convinced that the most promising young Eskimo men of any area were those who attended the mission schools, which taught anyone who wanted to learn without regard to age. These students eagerly grappled with language problems. They used paper and pencil, wholly new items in their experience, not only for schoolwork but for drawing.

The four Siberian herders Sheldon Jackson hired to accompany the first reindeer brought to mainland Alaska. Photograph by S. J. Call. Courtesy of Department of History, Presbyterian Church, U.S.A.

Because the mission teachers were the people most likely to know which Eskimos would most easily take to apprenticeship, Jackson felt that they were the logical ones to select trustworthy and able young men for this training. Small herds would be loaned to each mission station by the government to serve as tools for teaching reindeer herding.

Apprentice herders were to earn one female deer each year, along with its offspring. The female reproduces annually, beginning in her second year. At that rate, an Eskimo who had completed a five-year apprenticeship would start out with his own small herd. The intent was that a number of Eskimos would then form their animals into a larger herd, using ear marks for identification, and share herding responsibilities.

The annual *Reports* describe differences among the natives who came to learn the trade. Some came primarily to have the free food, clothing, and shelter, without seriously following orders and other disciplines. None was turned away before spring breakup, but many were refused a second season. It was thought that the Eskimos who showed themselves the best learners would demonstrate to other Eskimos and to outsiders the value of reindeer herding in the far north.

Early Problems

Cultural clashes occurred between the Eskimos and the Chukchis who were the chief herders and the herding instructors. Even though they had agreed to trade live deer, perhaps the Chukchis did not want the Alaskan reindeer project to succeed.

The Chukchis treated the deer harshly and were careless with the newborn fawns. Their method of milking the female was to lasso her and throw her down, with three men pinning her to the ground while the fourth milked her with thumb and finger. No wonder the flow of milk was practically nil! As we shall see, a very different picture emerged with the Lapp teachers.

After the first young Eskimos began training, the fledgling reindeer industry faced still other problems. Developing the industry was a matter of trial and error in many respects. Neither the whites in charge at Teller nor the Eskimos had experience raising domestic reindeer. With no pattern to follow, no long range planning was possible.

The first group of Siberian herders went back home on the last trip of the *Bear* that summer. One of them returned with three other herders. At the time there was no good alternative to accepting them. Their experience was needed to maintain the reindeer.

Another problem developed over keeping Teller Station open. At first, when contracts with Miner Bruce and Bruce Gibson ended June 30, 1893, the future looked secure. William T. Lopp, who was then at the American Missionary Association Mission at Cape Prince of Wales, accepted an appointment as the superintendent of Teller Station.

Lopp and his wife were well suited to work at the reindeer station. They had been living with the Eskimos at Wales for three years, as teachers and friends. They had learned the Eskimo language, and had gained many insights into their needs and outlook.

However, Lopp could not leave the Wales mission immediately. This problem was solved temporarily when supervision of the Teller Station was placed in the hands of two men from Captain Healy's crew. Then, shortly after Lopp was able to get to Teller, his partner back at the Wales mission was murdered by natives. The murderers were promptly caught by the villagers and put to death. However, the mission closed, and Lopp felt a responsibility to return there if his help was desired.

Sheldon Jackson, understanding Lopp's position, ran advertisements in many Scandinavian newspapers in the United States, seeking the services of Norwegian or Swedish men experienced in the Lapp style of reindeer herding. He received 250 responses.

Some of the letter writers were from the area referred to then as Lapland, the far north coastal regions of Norway, Sweden, and Finland. They described their experiences among the reindeer people of these areas. Some had lived with the nomadic herders.

According to those who wrote, the reindeer movement would be successful only with families from Lapland. Respondents also said that dogs trained in Lapland would be necessary.

All in all, Jackson must have been pleased with the information he received on reindeer herding. Now he needed to choose a superintendent for Teller Station who was familiar with Lapp herding.

William T. Lopp, who worked with Eskimos for many years, was a leading authority on reindeer throughout his life. Photograph in the 1895 *Report on Introduction of Domestic Reindeer into Alaska*.

William T. Lopp

William T. Lopp was 26, principal of the public school in his hometown of Valley City, Indiana, when he responded to a call for missionary teachers to Alaska. He met his co-worker, Harrison Thornton of Virginia, age 32, when they boarded the steamer for Alaska in San Francisco.

The two men were met by Sheldon Jackson in Port Clarence, Alaska. Jackson, Thornton, and Lopp laid the foundation for their mission school at Cape Prince of Wales on the very next day, July 4, 1890. The Wales school was the first to be built in northwest Alaska.

Building materials and school supplies had been delivered by a schooner the previous day. Sheldon Jackson had made all these arrangements from his office in the U.S. capital well in advance of his trip. Freight deliveries were made only once a year, due to ice and storm conditions in the Bering Sea, making it necessary to place orders six months to a year in advance of shipment. With the help of volunteers from Port Clarence, and carpenters from the *Bear* and from whaling vessels in the area, the building was ready for occupancy on July 12.

Lopp and Thornton continued their preparations for the school year. The population of the village was about 500, but only about 100 were in the village, all the others having gone to hunt and gather food for the winter. Still, when school opened in October, there were 138 pupils. Average daily attendance for the nine months was 113.

One of the greatest problems in school attendance was the lack of sunup and sundown. There were no clocks in the homes. When the schoolbell rang at 9 a.m. it was as dark as at 9 p.m. For generations the cultural patterns dictated time only according to the need for hunting and gathering in season. The long dark nights of winter relaxed into quiet family activities. Often the children came to school at the wrong time, and frequently arrived without breakfast. The first year was a very trying —but a learning—experience for the teachers as well as the students.

When Sheldon Jackson returned with the *Bear* in July, 1891, he was satisfied with the school's progress. Thornton returned home that year to report on the work in Alaska—and to find a bride. Lopp spent the winter of 1891-92 by himself in this Eskimo village. He showed sincere concern for the Eskimos, and won their respect and friendship. He became known by an Eskimo name that translated to "Tom the Good."

Thornton had not done as well. Being a moody person, with spells of depression, life among the Eskimos proved very difficult for him. He returned in the summer of 1892 with his new wife. He also brought Nellie Kittredge to keep her company. A month later Nellie became Mrs. William Lopp. The two couples shared teaching and preaching responsibilities.

On July 10, 1892, the *Bear* arrived at Cape Prince of Wales to take Mr. and Mrs. Lopp to Teller Reindeer Station, where Sheldon Jackson had assigned Lopp as superintendent. This stay was short-lived. When Thornton was killed, Lopp returned to the mission at Cape Prince of Wales.

Mr. and Mrs. Lopp learned the language and customs of their hosts. In the first distribution of reindeer from the government herd in Teller in 1894, Lopp was given charge of 119 reindeer. His ability to communicate with the Eskimos of his area, and to interpret the meaning of the program to them, gave him an important position in this new industry.

From 1894 to 1902 the herd increased rapidly. There were 75 fawns born in 1895, and each female reproduced when two years old. Lopp installed an "endless chain" system for rewarding apprentices. He allowed each apprentice $385 in food and clothing for five years, and at the end of that time gave him a bonus of six to ten reindeer, with their increase, as his own herd. Lopp gave instructions in keeping accounts and marking the deer. He and his wife also taught elementary reading, writing, and arithmetic.

William T. Lopp (*continued*)

In November 1897, events drew Lopp into one of the most critical and demanding chapters of his life. Eight whaling ships were caught in the ice near Point Barrow, and the men aboard were thought to be near starvation. (Chapter 7 recounts the dramatic rescue effort.)

Lopp's daily diary, kept while he was driving the 448 reindeer some 700 miles from Cape Prince of Wales to Point Barrow, gives vivid details of the hardships, both for the men and for the animals. He faithfully made entries regardless of weather and sometimes frozen fingers, face, and hands, and occasional snowblindness. (Appendix D, beginning on page 102, is an excerpt from Lopp's diary.)

The Lopp family moved to Seattle, Washington, in 1902. William Lopp continued to be active in Alaskan affairs. For 13 years he served as chief of the Alaska Division of the U.S. Bureau of Education, following in the footsteps of Sheldon Jackson, the man who brought him to Alaska in 1890. Lopp was later appointed Superintendent of Education for Alaska Natives. And until his death in 1939 he was recognized worldwide as an expert on the reindeer industry.

Nellie Kittredge Lopp

Mrs. Lopp was Nellie Kittredge, born in Glydon, Minnesota, in 1868. She was teaching in an institute for black children in Wilmington, North Carolina, when in 1892 she learned of an opening in Alaska missions. She was enthusiastic about the possibility of teaching Alaskan children.

Just two months after learning about the opening Nellie was one of five passengers on a steamer bound for Cape Prince of Wales in Alaska. Her lively and lengthy letters home described every aspect of the voyage. She justified the trip to her family by saying she would be a companion for the newly married Mrs. Harrison Thornton. In truth, she enjoyed traveling alone rather than with someone who would tell her what she should—or should not—do; or who would talk to her when she didn't want to listen.

Nellie arrived at Cape Prince of Wales in July 1892 and married William T. Lopp a month later. For ten years Nellie Lopp assisted her husband in teaching the Eskimos a better way of life. She bore six children during this time, often describing herself as giving more time to the Eskimo children than to her own family.

Nellie proved to be an excellent teacher and friend to the Eskimos. She revised the English reading text to reflect the local experience:

See the men and boys. What are they doing? They are herding deer. If all the men and boys sleep, the deer may run off. I like to look at a big herd of deer. The deer can draw a sled fast. I like deer meat and fat. Do you know how to herd deer? How many deer men or herders can you see? One, two, three . . .

When teaching the Sunday School lessons, she struggled to create interpretations that would have meaning within the Eskimo culture. Letters to her family went into great detail about her efforts at these adaptations.

When the thousands of prospectors came into the area seeking gold, Nellie and her husband were deeply concerned about the effect the miners would have on the Eskimos. The Lopps themselves filed on a few claims, but these did not amount to anything. Nellie wrote to her family that if they found any valuable gold so near that they could have it without neglecting their duties, then she felt it was meant for them.

She was content with her life. She found an expression that she adopted for herself: "We limit our wants to the things we are likely to get."

In 1902 the family moved to Seattle, where Nellie bore two more children.

5

Lapp Herders Come to Alaska

Among those who wrote letters in response to Jackson's advertisements, one man stood out: William A. Kjellmann. From the advice offered by Kjellmann and the other letter writers and from the experience with the Siberian herders, Jackson was convinced that it was also desirable to secure experienced herders from Lapland to handle the reindeer herds and to instruct the Eskimos. This would mean bringing their families and their trained dogs, as well as sleds and equipment.

Lapp herder on skis. Courtesy of University of Alaska Archives, Palmer Collection.

First Reindeer Superintendent

Born in Finmarken, northern Norway, William Kjellmann herded reindeer as soon as he was old enough. He continued in this work until he was 22 years old. Following that, he spent six years buying and selling reindeer and reindeer products. For three years he had been living in Madison, Wisconsin, with his family, and he had developed a good command of English. He was willing to help get the reindeer project started.

No sooner had Kjellmann been appointed the superintendent of Teller—a place he had not yet even seen—than he was asked to go to Lapland. He was to hire five families and their specially bred and trained dogs, and accompany them to Alaska.

Congress had not yet voted funds for the reindeer project. Fortunately, another $1,000 was donated to Jackson by his friends in the eastern United States to handle this trip. Kjellmann left for Lapland on February 16, 1894, just two days after his appointment.

This trip took Kjellmann back to northern Norway, where he knew herders and could speak their language. His big problem was convincing people who had never been south of the Arctic Circle in northern Europe to leave their familiar surroundings and move to faraway Alaska, with all of its unknowns.

Reindeer herders from Lapland and their families. Photographed in San Francisco before the final leg of their long journey to Alaska. Courtesy of Department of History, Presbyterian Church, U.S.A.

The Lapps' Long Journey

Kjellmann finally assembled a group of Lapps willing to go so long as they would have a minister of their faith in the new land. The group included:

    Per Aslaksen Rist, age 50

    Johan Speinsen Tornensis, age 35

        wife Margrethe, age 28

        Berit, 10 months

    Aslak Larsen Somby, age 48

        wife Britha, age 46

        Berit Anne, 11 years

    Mathis Aslaksen Eira, age 25

        wife Berit, age 37

        Aslek, 4 years

    Mikkel Josefsen Nakkila, age 32

        wife Berit, age 24

    Samuel Johnsen Kemi, age 46

        wife Kjersti, age 27

        Karen, 9 months

    Frederik Larsen, age 18.

On the first leg of their journey, the Lapps traveled by train. Their first train ride was a frightening experience. Every time the train whistle blew, their knuckles grew white as they grabbed the seats. Then, too, as they moved down from the mountains they knew so well, these northern people were in awe of the green pastures, and of farmers working in the fields.

Crossing the Atlantic made some of the Lapps quite seasick. One of their ten dogs died and was buried at sea. However, at last the travelers arrived at Ellis Island, New York. Once at this famous customs point, the greatest difficulty was not in checking the Lapps through customs, but their dogs. There was no documentation on the animals because there were no breeding stations or certificates in the land where these dogs came from. But Kjellmann managed to clear customs with all of his charges.

From New York, Kjellmann took them by train to his home in Madison, Wisconsin, where he had to finish up a few personal affairs. Here, Kjellmann's wife, daughter, and father joined the group.

The Kjellmann family (left) and Brevig family at Teller Reindeer Station, Alaska, 1895. Courtesy of Department of History, Presbyterian Church, U.S.A.

When they reached St. Paul, Minnesota, the Lapp families were pleased to be joined by Tollef Larson Brevig, a Lutheran minister, along with his wife Julia and their nine-month-old son.

A colorful group it was that headed west from St. Paul. The families from Lapland wore their distinctive national folk costume. The men had on brightly colored short jackets with yellow, red, and blue trimming, bloused trousers, and square hats with huge red pompons. From each man's belt hung a long knife.

The train trip across the continent was complicated by railroad washouts and other mishaps. However, the Kjellmanns, the Brevigs, and the Lapp families finally made it to Seattle, Washington, where they all boarded the steamer *Umatilla*, headed for San Francisco. They arrived in San Francisco on June 4. From then until they boarded the

ship for Alaska, a matter of thirteen days, the Lapps explored the big city. They were escorted everywhere by the manager of the Sailor's Home, where they stayed.

At last the travelers landed at Teller Reindeer Station on July 31, 1894. And soon the Lapps began their work as herders and instructors for the Eskimos.

Kjellmann and T. L. Brevig made a strong combination as Superintendent and Assistant Superintendent of Teller Reindeer Station. Although it is uncertain how much of the language Kjellmann learned, Brevig soon mastered Eskimo. Between them the two men spoke the languages and knew the background of the people they worked with.

Details of life and events during the first year, July 1, 1894 through June 30, 1895, appear in a journal kept at Teller. (Excerpts from the journal are reproduced as Appendix C, beginning on page 95.)

Lapp Teachers, Eskimo Apprentices

The Lapps had three-year contracts, after which they would have the choice to remain or return to Lapland. Besides receiving food, clothing, and shelter, and 1200 kroner per year (equivalent to $321.60, U.S. currency), the Lapps were permitted to utilize any animals they needed for food and clothing. This last was difficult for the Eskimo apprentices to accept because they were not allowed to slaughter reindeer.

This difference in treatment added to resentment instilled among Eskimos by bootleggers who resented the prohibition of their products among natives. White men, denied ownership of deer, which they foresaw as profitable, also encouraged Eskimo dissatisfaction. However, Superintendent Kjellmann explained why the Eskimos were so disposed, and urged the Lapps to be patient teachers.

It was not long until the Eskimos recognized the knowledge and experience of their trainers, and good working relationships were established. The skill and gentleness of the Lapps in handling the deer at fawning time was impressive. In 1894, out of the 186 born under supervision of the Siberian herders at Teller Station, 41 fawns had been lost. In the spring of 1895, under Lapp care, only 15 fawns were lost out of the 223 born.

Freighting with Reindeer. (Eskimo Drawing)

Courtesy of National Archives.

6

Reindeer Herds Multiply

With the reindeer thriving, the distribution of reindeer from the nucleus herd at Teller Reindeer Station began. In 1894 a herd of 100 reindeer was driven 60 miles northwest to the mission at Cape Prince of Wales.

Jackson wrote a letter to William T. Lopp who had returned to Wales from Teller and was in charge of the mission. In the letter, reproduced separately in this chapter, he outlined procedures and responsibilities of the mission and listed details of the annual report required by the government.

For his own part, Lopp decided that only Eskimos would handle the government deer under his supervision. His decision probably resulted in part from observing the clashes between cultures at Teller. He also wanted to develop his own system of herding and apprenticeship based on his understanding of the Eskimos who had gathered around the mission at Wales.

At the same time Jackson was interested in pushing ahead with the reindeer project, he recognized that white men, with their ingenuity for private enterprise, could easily interfere with the Eskimos' beginning reindeer industry. He wrote to the Department of the Interior:

. . . if white men are allowed to establish herds, they will not get into the hands of the natives, and the main object in the enterprise will be defeated.

I would, therefore, recommend that legislation be secured for the protection of the Government in the laudable effort to introduce domesticated reindeer as the commencement of civilization among the Eskimo of Alaska. [1]

Nobody followed through on this recommendation of Jackson's.

Reindeer calves suckle through their first summer. Courtesy of Glenbow Archives, Calgary, Alberta.

Charley Antisarlook's Herd

When the mission station at Wales received its herd, the Eskimo apprentices at Teller Station began to think they would never be allowed to own any reindeer. To show good faith, a herd of 113 reindeer was loaned to Charley Antisarlook and three promising apprentices early in 1895. The herd consisted of 21 males, 83 females, and 9 fawns, a proportion considered good for a new herd.

The new reindeer herd was driven to Charley Antisarlook's home grounds at Point Rodney, near what is now Nome. Antisarlook was placed in charge of this herd. Working with him were Soovawhasie, Iziksic, Koktoak, and Iuppik, who had completed part of their apprenticeship and had earned a few deer.

When fawning time arrived, Lapp herders from Teller Reindeer Station went to assist with the Point Rodney herd. At the yearly count in July of 1896, 218 reindeer were counted, including 43 fawns born in the spring. There would have been eleven more in the summer count had they not been killed by an avalanche that came down the mountain where they were feeding.

Charley's loan specified that 100 reindeer would be returned to the government herd after five years, and he and his partners would keep the increase to begin their own herds. They were off to a good start.

Demand for Reindeer Services

In his *Report* to Congress for the year 1896, Jackson said that the government herd at Teller Reindeer Station numbered 423. That winter there were also the Wales herd of 253, Charley Antisarlook's herd of 218, and two other herds within range of easy oversight by Teller: 50 at St. James Mission on the Yukon River and 50 at the Swedish Mission at Golovin Bay.

The reindeer were trained to pull sleds. Courtesy of Alaska Historical Library, Juneau.

Still, requests for reindeer kept coming in, partly due to the discovery of gold in Alaska. The year 1895 brought increased activity in gold mining along the Yukon River. A demand grew for freighting supplies of miners and carrying passengers and mail along the Yukon from coastal ports. Dog teams were used, but such high prices were charged for their use that the more economical reindeer teams became popular. Lapps and apprentices were kept busy training sled deer and providing services to the miners and to the troops at St. Michael.

Reindeer Transport Troubles

No reindeer were transported from Siberia in 1896 and 1897. Miner Bruce was contracted to purchase deer and was going to ship them to Alaska on the *Bear* in 1896. However, he was unable to fulfill the contract because during that year the *Bear* was occupied with policing against illegal sealing on and near the Pribilof Islands in the Bering Sea.

Jackson sought other means of securing and transporting reindeer from Siberia. His

Department of the Interior,

Bureau of Education,

ALASKA DIVISION,
On Board U.S. R. Cutter "Bear"
August 18th, 1894

Mr W. T. Lopp.
Superintendent of the American Missionary
Association Station. Cape Prince of Wales.

Sir

In the introduction of reindeer into Alaska, the United States Bureau of Education greatly desires the Cooperation and assistance of the Missionaries of all the Churches in Alaska. Being the most intelligent and disinterested friends of the natives, it naturally looks to them as the best agents through whom to reach the native population. From their position & work, having learned the Character & needs of the people, they are able to most wisely plan and carry out methods for transferring the ownership of the deer from the Government to the natives in such a manner as will best facilitate the Reindeer industry. The Government further realizes the fact that the Men, who most completely come under Mission influence Civilization & Education are the Coming men of affairs among their own people and therefore are the best men to lead off in a new movement.

William T. Lopp was teacher and reindeer superintendent at Cape Prince of Wales when Sheldon Jackson wrote him this letter. Creating detailed instructions for the beginning of an industry that would include many

2

As the wide & general distribution of the reindeer will both save the people, among whom they work, from extinction, and place them upon a plane of independent self support, the Missionaries have a direct and personal interest with the Government in the work.

To secure this cooperation of the Missionaries, the U.S. Bureau of Education proposes from time to time to furnish herds of reindeer to all the Mission Stations in North Western and Central Alaska, that through them more Natives may be trained to care for the deer and when so trained receive the loan of a sufficient number to commence a private herd.

As a beginning in this direction, it affords me much pleasure to turn over to you as the representative of the Congregational Mission at Cape Prince of Wales one hundred head of deer, with the single condition that upon the 1st of July each year you, or your successors, make out an annual report of the progress of the herd, giving the numbers born, dying or killed, the number and character of herders & apprentices or learners, what steps are being taken & with what success to get your people to take them up, the condition of private herds in your neighborhood and what experiments you may have made towards improved methods of harnessing, milking and handling the deer together with the results of the same. "This annual report will be mailed to the General Agent of Education in Alaska. U.S. Bureau of Education. Washington. D.C. ."

Wishing you great Success I remain
Yours Truly
Sheldon Jackson
General Agent.

inexperienced people with untried skills must have been a great challenge. The reindeer project evolved by trial and error as time passed. Courtesy of Stratton Library Archives, Sheldon Jackson College, Sitka, Alaska.

Watchful herders kept the reindeer from ranging far and wide, resulting in quiet herds and tame animals. Courtesy of University of Alaska Archives, Palmer Collection.

Report for 1897 describes the final attempt to place purchasing agents in Siberia. During the summer a small frame house was erected and four men stayed there with barter goods to purchase up to 800 deer during the winter months. These reindeer were supposed to be on the coast in the spring of 1898, waiting to be transported to Teller Station. Apparently jealousies and feuds broke out among the Siberian villages, preventing further trading and endangering the lives of the agents. The agents fled on a whaling boat in July of 1898. In 1898 just 167 reindeer were transported.

Newspaper accounts raised questions about this episode. According to a September 4, 1898 article in *The Examiner*, a San Francisco newspaper, agents John W. Kelly and Conrad Seim had been given thousands of dollars worth of trade goods to purchase reindeer in Siberia.

When the Del Norte *(chartered to transport 800 reindeer from the Siberian Coast to Port Clarence) arrived Kelly and Seim were gone. They had taken the whaler* Alexander *and gone into the Arctic. They left word for Sheldon Jackson that they had purchased 900 deer and had been compelled to leave because their lives were in danger and provisions had run short. Arriving at St. Lawrence Bay Jackson sent for the herders and demanded the Government's deer. After much delay the Siberians drove down three or four herds. Out of the bunch 167 bore the government mark. The count was short 633, and, according to the statements of agents Kelly and Seim, the Government has been cheated to that extent. The natives say it was the other men. They claim that Kelly and Seim used the Government trading goods to purchase whalebone and furs for themselves, instead of reindeer for their Government. The natives declare that on the* Alexander *the two men took a valuable shipment of such things.*

At all events it appears strangely coincident that Kelly and Seim should have reached Port Townsend Friday morning on the schooner Compeer *from Point Hope. It is also of interest to note that the* Compeer *had whalebone and furs from the* Alexander.

Meanwhile, it is reported, Kelly and Seim, whom Mr. Jackson would no doubt like to meet, have gone to San Francisco.

Although few reindeer were obtained from Siberia during 1897 and 1898, the reindeer gained widespread attention in Alaska among natives and non-natives alike. Two separate expeditions, described in the next two chapters, proved the durability and usefulness of the reindeer.

7

The Rescue of Stranded Whalers

On November 15, 1897, the Secretary of the U.S. Treasury telegraphed Captain Francis Tuttle, commanding officer of the *Bear*, reporting that eight whaling vessels were icebound in the Arctic Ocean somewhere near Point Barrow, and that the 265 persons thought to be on board the ships were probably in dire distress.

Captain Tuttle, who had taken over command of the *Bear* from Captain Healy in 1896, had just returned from the annual six-month cruise in the Arctic waters. By order of the President and under direction of the Secretary of the Treasury, the *Bear* was rapidly prepared and with a crew of volunteers left Port Townsend in a blinding snowstorm to go to the aid of the whaling vessel crews.

Adapting the Rescue Plan

The 1898 *Report* to Congress on the reindeer industry includes considerable detail on the Point Barrow expedition. A number of the participants wrote accounts of the rescue, which was planned by Captain Tuttle and others experienced in the Arctic. Among the planners and those who volunteered for the dangerous trip were Lieutenant D. H. Jarvis, E. P. Bertholf, and surgeon S. J. Call.

The plan called for putting supplies ashore as far north as possible and sending them overland from there to the shipwrecked sailors. Lieutenant Jarvis would also drive reindeer from the herds along the coast.

The *Bear* had to fight ice formations once she passed through Dutch Harbor in the Aleutian chain and headed into the Bering Sea. Mush ice, then floe ice was solidifying so fast that she could only move at five miles per hour. Finally, for fear of becoming permanently fast in the ice, course was changed. The overland party was put ashore on Cape Vancouver, several hundred miles farther south than had been planned.

When the ship anchored near the village of Tununok, the local trader and a party of Eskimos came aboard. Learning of the relief expedition, these people offered to guide Jarvis as far as St. Michael, on the south side of Norton Sound. So supplies and men were put ashore, and the *Bear* returned to Dutch Harbor, Unalaska, for the winter.

Jarvis and four other men, including Dr. Call, started out on December 18 with dog teams pulling sleds loaded with relief supplies. Two days later, two of the teams gave out. While the rest of the party secured new dog teams and pushed ahead with the provisions, a portion of which they would leave for the men following with reindeer, Jarvis and Call set out to procure reindeer. The plan was for the group with supplies to cross Kotzebue Sound and meet up with reindeer herds from the Nome area.

Jarvis and Call reached the herd that was being driven from Teller to the new Eaton Station, with Dr. Kittilsen in charge. At their request, Kittilsen and two of the apprentices took the two men to Teller, where they prepared for the next leg of their journey. Kittilsen then left to catch up with the government herd moving to Eaton. Jarvis and Call went on toward the herds at Cape Prince of Wales and at Point Rodney, near Cape Nome.

At Wales, Tautook, one of the Eskimo herders, agreed to help drive the reindeer that Jarvis would get from other herds. The next day, reindeer sled teams took the two of them to the herd at Point Rodney.

Two Reindeer Herds

The Cape Nome reindeer herd represented a living for the whole Eskimo village. To part with the herd might mean starvation before spring. Mary Antisarlook, Charley's wife, put her feelings quite clearly:

Tell Mr. Jarvis we are very sorry for the people at Point Barrow and we want to help them, but we hate to see our deer go, because we are poor and

---

The Antisarlooks

Charley Antisarlook, an Eskimo hunter, was matched with Mary by her parents, sometime in the 1880s. Mary, born to an Eskimo woman and a Russian trader, was raised by her mother in the traditional ways of the Eskimo.

When Sheldon Jackson needed an interpreter for dealing with Siberian reindeer men, he was told of Mary, who lived in Sinruk near Nome. She could speak a Siberian dialect and worked as Sheldon Jackson's interpreter in the 1890s. She and her husband received reindeer in payment.

Charley earned deer during an apprenticeship at Teller Reindeer Station, becoming one of the first Eskimo herders in Alaska. In the winter of 1897-1898, he took the growing Nome herd and went with the rescue mission to Point Barrow as chief herder. The original number of reindeer plus what would have been their natural increase were replaced by the government the following year.

Mary became sole owner of their herd in 1900 when Charley died in the measles epidemic. Jackson's 1901 *Report* describes Mary's herd as numbering 360. She owned 272 and the rest of the herd belonged to other family members. White men, passing through the country from one mine to another, killed some of the herd. To get away from this trouble the herd was moved to the Unalakleet area.

Even before Charley's death, Mary had started to adopt children. Sinruk Mary adopted 11 children in her lifetime. They all worked for her until they got married or left home. She was a strict manager and took good care of the animals. She prospered. She was known as the "Reindeer Queen," and at one time it was estimated that she had 1,500 reindeer.

Sinruk Mary continued her traditional role of preparing fish, seal, and whale and making skin clothing for her large household. She married a second time and continued to expand her family. By the 1930s the reindeer herds had dwindled. Mary's wealth was gone.

In her old age Sinruk Mary shared her memories with all who would listen. One attentive listener was her granddaughter, Esther Agibinik, who spent many hours combing her grandmother's hair and listening as Mary told traditional stories and described the skills she learned as a girl. She told of her life as interpreter for Sheldon Jackson during the early years of the Alaskan reindeer industry. Sinruk Mary's last years were spent at Unalakleet, where she died in 1949.

our people in the village are poor, and in the winter when we cannot get seals we kill a deer, and this helps us through the hard times. If we let our deer go, what are we to do? Antisarlook and I have not enough without them to live upon. [2]

Nonetheless, after consultation among themselves, the Antisarlooks and other villagers came to a difficult decision: they would give up their deer. Charley Antisarlook agreed to help drive the deer north.

In the Cape Nome herd there were 138 reindeer, 22 of them belonging to Eskimos other than the Antisarlooks. Arrangements were made to return 220 reindeer the following year, which would allow for an increase of 82 fawns.

At the Wales station there was no difficulty in explaining the need for the reindeer.

Mary Antisarlook took over her husband Charley's herd after he died during the 1900 epidemic. She became known as the "Reindeer Queen" as she and her extended family developed their large herd. Photograph in the 1901 *Report on Introduction of Domestic Reindeer into Alaska.*

In fact, Lopp and six of the Eskimo herders—Sokwena, Ootenna, Netaxite, Kivyeargruk, Stuk, and Keok—readily joined in with the relief expedition.

There were 301 deer in the herd at Wales. It was agreed that the same number of deer would be returned to Wales the following season together with what would be expected as natural increase from that number.

Jarvis and Call had decided to drive separate herds. They would meet up at various predetermined points. These rendezvous were probably meant as a way of checking on how each was doing in the stormy weather on treacherous terrain. They also would share supply caches along the way.

Men and reindeer had to battle raging Arctic storms as they advanced to meet each other. The deer were scattered by the storms and time was lost in gathering them back together. As a result, the two herds missed the first rendezvous, although only by a narrow margin. The two herds finally came together at the beginning of February. Eighteen of the deer were already broken to harness and were reserved for transportation.

To save many miles of travel, the relief expedition then crossed the frozen, but dangerous Kotzebue Sound. The hummocks of piled-up ice at times made it necessary to chop "steps" for the deer to cross over.

Success

Finally, at noon on March 26, 1898, Jarvis caught sight of the tall mast of the *Belvedere*, 12 miles away across the ice. He reached Point Barrow three days later. The reindeer arrived the following day, having travelled hundreds of miles over untracked regions in the depths of a harsh Arctic winter.

Letters written by Jarvis and by Tuttle, which appear in the 1898 *Report* on reindeer, describe the relief expedition. A diary kept by Lopp gives details of the daily hardships faced

Taking supplies across the ice to wrecked whalers, Point Barrow, Alaska. Photograph in the 1898 *Report on Introduction of Domestic Reindeer into Alaska.*

by both man and beast. He faithfully made entries regardless of weather, sometimes frozen fingers, face, and hands, and occasional snowblindness. (Selections from Lopp's diary appear as Appendix D, beginning on page 102.)

Having done his part, Lopp returned to Cape Prince of Wales, going by dog team. Ample provisions cached along the way northbound made his return south easy. He reached home May 5, having been away just over three months.

Jarvis stayed on at Point Barrow, where the stranded whalers were already being helped by the three leading white residents: Dr. H. R. Marsh, Presbyterian missionary; Mr. Charles D. Brower, agent of the Liebes

Whaling Company; and Mr. McIlhenny (no first name given), a scientist making an Arctic collection. Brower had been issuing rations from his store. Marsh had been providing medical services and health care to prevent scurvy and other diseases. All the houses had taken in as many men as could possibly be accommodated.

Salvage from the icebound ships had been laboriously hauled across miles of frozen ocean. Some of the men stayed aboard ships that were solidly frozen in the ice. They were quite safe until the spring breakup would start shifting the ice. Graphic descriptions of the eventual destruction of some of the ships and the release of others are in the records.[3]

The Eskimos of Point Barrow had gone into the surrounding countryside to get wild game both for themselves and the whalers. Wild game and fish were plentiful that season. Reports state that Eskimos brought in 15,100 pounds of meat and more than 8,500 pounds of fish.

After Jarvis arrived, the reindeer men under his direction brought in another 3,000 pounds of meat, some of it from as far away as 230 miles. From the domestic reindeer that had been driven north, 60 were used for food along the way. Some others strayed or were lost to storms. During the rest of the winter, 180 male deer were killed for food.

The determination of the men on the rescue drive was matched by that of Nellie Lopp. When she was urged to go to Teller Station, a distance of 75 miles, to stay with the Brevigs until her husband's return, Nellie said "No." Rather than brave the dangerous trip she preferred to stay in her village—the only English-speaking person in a community of 500 Eskimos.

This reindeer shows the harness marks for pulling a sled. Note the large lateral hooves that spread on soft ground or snow—like snowshoes. Both sexes have antlers. Courtesy of National Archives.

New Reindeer Interest

The reindeer drive passed through and near many Eskimo villages on the way from Cape Nome and Cape Prince of Wales to Point Barrow. The appearance of the reindeer in the distance at times brought out hunters with their various equipment for securing food. The many reindeer wearing bells helped to make it clear that this was not a migrating wild herd. Still, the herders had to be in readiness to protect the reindeer and explain that these were domestic animals.

As a result of the new contacts, Eskimos who had not heard of the reindeer project before became very interested. The question heard again and again was, "How soon can we have a herd for our village?"

8

Reindeer to Miners on the Yukon

The summer of 1897 saw an unusually low flow of water in the Yukon River, which was the principle traffic lane for freight steamers going to the interior of the country. Because of the low water, supplies that were meant for the miners had to be unloaded at Fort St. Michael at the mouth of the Yukon, 1,500 miles to the south and west of the main mining camps.

As winter approached, the panic-stricken miners looked to the government for help. Initial plans were made to use the trained reindeer on the Seward Peninsula to haul supplies to the miners by sled. But then the call for help came from the whalers caught in the ice at Point Barrow, and all plans were changed.

Overseas Organizing

In December of 1897, Sheldon Jackson was directed by the Secretary of the Interior to report to the Secretary of War for temporary duty. His assignment was to go immediately to Norway and Sweden where he was to hire drivers and purchase 500 harness-trained reindeer, together with sleds. These he was instructed to transport to the United States so that supplies could be hauled into the Yukon Valley. Lieutenant D. B. Devore was appointed to go along as disbursing officer.

When Jackson received his orders, Kjellmann was again in Norway, having gone with those Lapps who had come to Alaska in 1894 to train the Eskimo herders and at the end of their three-year contract had chosen to return home. Kjellmann had been directed to find other Lapps who would come to the United States with plans to become citizens.

Jackson crossed the Atlantic by steamship and arrived at Liverpool, England, early Christmas morning. Transferring funds to Kjellmann in Norway was a major undertaking. And so was arranging for a ship to cross the Atlantic with the 500 reindeer and more than 50 Lapps, plus all the sleds and other equipment. Finally, Jackson had to make sure that there would be at least 250 tons of the needed reindeer moss ready for shipment, reindeer food for which Kjellmann had done preliminary scouting.

Because only Kjellmann knew the country and the herders, he set off to purchase the required reindeer. Each herd would have only three to six trained deer to spare so he had to travel from herd to herd over hundreds of miles of snow-covered country. Since the sun does not appear above the horizon from the middle of November until late January, all this travel took place during darkness.

Kjellmann successfully completed the

purchases and arranged for the reindeer to be driven to one location. In the end, three major drives from widely separated points were brought together at Bosekop, arriving within just a few hours of one another. This description appears in the 1898 *Report*:

On February 1 the little village of Bosekop awoke from its Arctic night to unusual stir and activity as the Lapps and deer came pouring in long lines over the hill into the village, filling up Market Square. The hundreds of Lapps . . . those that were going away and those that had come to see them off, greeting old friends and meeting new ones, the unpacking of sleds and preparations for embarkation, all made a picture never to be forgotten. All was bustle and excitement. By night everything was ready for the arrival of the steamship, and the first part of the expedition–the purchase of reindeer, sleds, and harness, together with the securing of competent drivers, was an accomplished success. [4]

Another Long Journey

During the stormy Atlantic crossing, the ship's figurehead was torn from the iron prow and swept away by the sea. But the reindeer were good travelers. Only one of the 539 on board died—and that one died of injuries from fighting.

The Lapps were organized into teams that tended the deer regularly. Diligent in caring for the deer, the Lapps carefully gathered falling snow in pails for the deer to eat when the fresh water supply ran out.

The trip across the United States by train was without incident. But the delay of nine days in Seattle while waiting for a ship to take them to Alaska was disastrous. To save moss for the sea voyage from Seattle to Alaska, the deer were taken to city parks and placed on grass. This change of diet caused several to die in Seattle and more to die soon thereafter.

Sheldon Jackson (second from right) with reindeer at Haines, Alaska. Courtesy of Elizabeth Hakkinen, Sheldon Museum, Haines.

In total, at least a dozen reindeer died from eating food they were not used to.

In late March 1898, 526 reindeer, the Lapp herders, and the herders' equipment were landed on the beach at Haines, Alaska, the nearest port to the troubled miners on the Yukon. There everyone waited for instructions for the next part of the journey.

Although the instructions were mailed in plenty of time from Skagway to the officer in charge at Dyea, just six miles away, they were delayed nearly a week. Meanwhile, just two days after the arrival at Haines, an early thaw took the ice out of the Chilkat River, making a drive to the moss higher in the valley impossible.

As a result of the delays in communication and warm weather, the reindeer had to be fed dried alfalfa, the only food available. This greatly undermined their health. Within three days they started dying. The Lapps found moss on a mountain 12 miles away and drove the weakened herd there. Several animals died on the way.

When instructions finally arrived, the herders drove their charges through Klukwan, and advanced to the head of the Thleheena River, where a little moss was found. This moss soon gave out. The herders and the deer slowly progressed up the Chilkat Valley. The struggle continued until the north summit was finally reached in the first week of May. Only 144 deer had survived the trip.

Kjellmann had been instructed to accompany the expedition only until it was headed into the interior. He then returned to Port Townsend, Washington, and Hedley E. Redmyer took over. When Redmyer began to fear that the provisions for the men would not hold out, he sent a group of men back to Haines in order to take a steamer to Seattle and locate Kjellmann. Six of the men stayed to continue with the reindeer to Circle City: Per Johannessen Hatta, Per Nilsen Siri, Klemet Person Boini, Aners Aslaksen Bahr, Hans Andersen Siri, and Emil Kjeldberg.

The sleds brought by the Lapps, called "pulkas," look like small boats. Photograph in the 1898 *Report on Introduction of Domestic Reindeer into Alaska.*

By 1898, T. L. Brevig had maintained a Lutheran mission next to Teller Reindeer Station for four years. He acted as teacher and minister, librarian, dispenser of medicines, and sometimes station manager.

In April of 1898 Brevig also began ministering to 60 Eskimos in a village called Nook (renamed Teller in 1901), seven miles across Port Clarence Bay. As Brevig wrote for the annual *Report*:

The winter had been very severe. The results of fishing through the ice were very meager, especially during the three coldest months. The food situation bordered on famine. This I did not fully realize until one morning in March when a widow was brought to our station who suffered from a wound in her throat. Those who brought her told me that she had attempted suicide because she had been without food for many days. They also reported that there was scarcely any food left in the entire village. By a hurried investigation I found that this report was true. Already two children and one old woman were dead from starvation. My limited personal supply was indeed insufficient for feeding a hundred extra mouths.

For several years the Government had stored two tons of bran at the station, to be used for feeding the reindeer. But the reindeer would not eat the bran. By taking this bran and distributing it amongst the natives, we saved their lives until the fish returned to the coastal waters again in April. A little flour also was given to those who were weakest.

The Government demanded pay for that which I had distributed, because nothing could be given away without Congressional action. Five dollars paid the bill.

By this time the snow was so far gone that sleds were of no further use. They were carefully stacked and marked as property of the U.S. Army. It was now necessary to use the reindeer as pack animals. They were given time to regain strength while the men prepared pack saddles and divided their provisions into twenty-five pound bags.

Lake Klukshu, in the Northwest Territory, Canada, was reached on September 1. From here on the journey was once more on snow, and the men built sleds on which to carry provisions.

On February 25, 1899, the U.S. Army's overland expedition reached its destination —Circle City on the Yukon River—with 114 reindeer. By this time any emergency along the Yukon was long past. Jackson was instructed to settle all accounts and salaries, and to transfer unused provisions to the Department of the Interior for Alaska's education program.

Adjusting to Circumstances

To avoid the expense of driving the surviving reindeer to Eaton Station 1,000 miles westward, an exchange was worked out. The Circle City animals would move to the mouth of the Tanana River instead of the ones at Golovin Bay, which would go to Eaton.

In the end, the reindeer from Golovin were driven to Point Rodney, just 80 miles to the west. These deer were a partial replacement for those the government had borrowed from Antisarlook for the rescue of the whalers at Point Barrow.

No longer needed for the U.S. military relief operation, the 67 Lapps, Finns, and Norwegians and their families who had crossed the Atlantic to help with the relief of miners were transferred from the War Department to the Interior Department. They arrived at Eaton Reindeer Station, Unalakleet, at the end of July 1898.

9

Of Gold and Reindeer

The years 1898 and 1899 brought Alaska into the news headlines time and again. The whalers caught in the Arctic ice, the miners threatened with starvation in the Yukon Valley, and the hectic race to gold over the Chilkat Pass by men and women and their pack animals made ongoing stories that caught the public's imagination.

Tucked into the exciting stories was the portrayal of the gentle reindeer to the rescue. The reindeer industry was ready to meet these new challenges.

Reindeer were popular with gold-seekers who used them as pack animals. Photograph in the 1899 *Report on Introduction of Domestic Reindeer into Alaska*.

Nome Gold Rush

Gold was discovered on the Snake River near Nome on the Seward Peninsula late in the fall of 1898. When the news of the latest gold strike reached other mining districts, men rushed to the Golovin Bay area, and to the "Gold Coast" of Nome.

Eaton became the main winter crossroads for miners, traders, and mail carriers between Dawson, the Yukon Valley, and Nome. Hundreds of miners stopped at Eaton overnight, many needing medical attention. There were no doctors except at reindeer stations like Eaton. In addition to accidents and illness, there were many cases of frostbite among those who arrived unprepared for the long dark cold winter. Kjellmann's daily log book at Eaton shows subzero temperatures from mid-November to mid-March, with a low of −40 on February 17.

Reindeer proved useful on the Seward Peninsula. They were the draft animals of choice to haul mail and freight supplies for the miners. There was also a demand for reindeer to transport the military personnel that were needed to keep order among the ill-prepared miners in a region with insufficient supplies and shelter.

The gold towns provided a ready market for reindeer meat. In fact, demand outran the limited supply during the winter of 1899-1900. Meat was imported from Siberia to help feed the 2,500 people then at Nome.

Private Reindeer Enterprises

The rush of fortune hunters to Alaska's golden shores brought with it many varieties of entrepreneurs. Supplies of all kinds had to be distributed in a land where no such distribution had existed in the past. With visions of establishing their own reindeer services, several "outsiders" attempted to procure reindeer. Sheldon Jackson described some of these efforts in his 1898 *Report*:

The sudden influx of large numbers of miners into central Alaska, and the difficulty of procuring supplies and provisions at the mining camps, called public attention to the necessity of introducing the reindeer as a factor in freighting and transportation. During the years when natives had occasion to travel from village to village their journeys were comparatively short and time was no object, consequently it made no difference whether they were a week or a month on the road, and dog teams served a useful purpose. So during the days of the fur trade the few fur traders in the country with their homes on the river, supplied with provisions by an annual trip of the steamer, could manage to get along comfortably with dog transportation. But in the increased and more rapid development of the country the need of better transportation facilities was recognized. The experiments of the Government had already demonstrated the value of the reindeer, and three or four private enterprises were at once started, the details of which have been difficult to obtain. From newspaper reports I glean that a Mr. G. Lewis of Montreal, acting in the interest of the Reindeer Transportation Company of Vancouver, shipped 42 reindeer from Norway on the steamship Hecla, *reaching New York February 1, 1898. They were consigned to a Mr. J. G. Scroggs. Seven died on the trip across the ocean, and 29 in crossing the continent. But 6 lived to reach Skagway, and of those but 2 reached Dawson.*

At Skagway I was informed that in November last Mr. David O'Neil, an Arizona miner, before going into the Yukon, visited Norway to procure a herd of reindeer for use at the mines. Not finding in eastern Lapland as large deer as he wanted, he continued up the coast to Tromsoe, then traveled into the interior across Norway and Sweden to Archangel, Russia, on the White Sea; from thence 180 miles north-east to Petchora Bay, Arctic Russia, where he is said to have found reindeer weighing from 500 to 600 pounds, trained both to hauling and packing. He purchased a herd of 2,000 head, costing about $12 apiece. With 34 selected deer he started for Hamburg, Germany, a journey of 1800 miles across the country. Twenty-three days were consumed in crossing the Atlantic, during which time a number of them died; others died in crossing the continent, so that when Skagway was reached only 1 deer out of the 34 was left, and that one died before he could be gotten off the wharf.

The poor success in transporting the 34 deer so discouraged him that he telegraphed to Russia to sell the remainder of the 2,000 that he had purchased. It is to be regretted that those enterprises were not more successful, as the deer are so greatly needed in Alaska. The failure, however, was not due to any insuperable difficulties in the way of transporting them from Lapland or to any inability of the reindeer to endure long voyages, as was proven when, a month later than Mr. O'Neil's expedition, the United States commissioner to Lapland transported 539 reindeer from Lapland, twenty-six days at sea and across the continent to Seattle, with the loss of but one.

I have been informed that in the above private expeditions sufficient moss was not brought with the deer, but an attempt was made to accustom them to live on hay and grain while en route.

The Nome gold rush benefited the reindeer industry. It also caused a new problem. It became difficult to keep the experienced herders from northern Europe involved with the government reindeer.

Some Lapps left the government reindeer service when their contracts were up and hired out the services of themselves and their reindeer. Many of the Lapps, Finns, and Norwegians who arrived at Eaton Station in 1899 were attracted to the gold mines, and were released from government service. Several families returned to Norway.

Jafet Lindeberg was one of three men who first discovered gold near Cape Nome; he left the reindeer service in mid-1898. Seeing his success, others abandoned herding to stake claims. The legal entanglements of non-citizens among the claims led to bitter battles—both physical and in the courts.

Fleet-Footed Mail Service

The station post office at Eaton became the distributing point for mail going north to Kotzebue, south to St. Michael, west to Golovin, Nome, Teller, and Cape Prince of Wales, and east to the Yukon Valley, Dawson, and on to the States.

In 1899 Jackson secured the establishment of the first reindeer postal route—from St. Michael on the coast of the Bering Sea to Kotzebue, north of the Arctic Circle. This meant three round trips during winter, each trip covering more than 1,000 miles of trackless tundra.

Reindeer were used to furnish winter mail service to all the people who had come to the Nome area looking for gold. Reindeer, which moved quickly across frozen tundra, seemed ideal for Arctic Alaska in wintertime.

Mary Andrewuk of Unalakleet with a reindeer packed for travel. Courtesy of National Archives.

Mail carriers. Courtesy of National Archives.

The U.S. Post Office Department entered into a contract with Kjellmann to carry the mail twice monthly during the winter between Eaton Station and Nome. Four trips were made with deer and sleds after February. It was reported that:

On the second trip the reindeer passed dogs and a bicycle that had passed Eaton 2 days before the deer started; reached Nome, rested 30 hours, and started on the return trip before the dog-team arrived. [5]

Later, several new routes were established by the post office. One route covered a distance of about 650 miles, from Kotzebue to Point Barrow by way of Point Hope. The first round trip was made with a reindeer team, with no relief teams along the way. This proved too fatiguing for the deer, so dog teams with relays along the way were used until it was possible to set up reindeer relay stations.

The reindeer could travel for 30 to 50 miles with a sled carrying 200 or 300 pounds. Reindeer relay stations would be needed about every 50 miles along the coast and along the Yukon, Koyukuk, and Kuskokwim rivers and far into the interior where traders and miners worked and lived. The plan for developing chains of stations is described further in Chapter 12.

A large number of young steers were trained to harness and many sled deer were furnished to the mail carriers. A number of pulkas, or Lapp reindeer sleds, and sets of harness were made for the use of Eaton Station and also for other stations.

Eskimo Herd at Teller

In December of 1899, Dr. Francis H. Gambell, who had come to Alaska from Iowa, reported to Jackson after an inspection tour of reindeer herds. He assured Jackson that the original idea and purpose of bringing domestic reindeer to Alaska was being realized, and had very good prospects for the future. His view of the future may well have been that surely the role of the reindeer industry would continue as Alaska was developed.

Gambell was particularly impressed by the herd in the area of the old reindeer station at Teller—a herd owned and cared for by Eskimos who had served as apprentices. He wrote that this herd was in as good condition as any of the other herds.

10

A Growing Industry

While the daring rescue expeditions and new gold discoveries in the northland made exciting news stories in the States, the woes and triumphs of the growing reindeer industry were less well publicized. Managing the new industry certainly was not easy. Frequent management changes occurred at Teller Reindeer Station. Nonetheless, the reindeer meant for the benefit of the Eskimos multiplied and new herds were established.

Events at Teller

Teller Reindeer Station was managed by a number of different men during the years 1892 through 1898. This is not surprising. Few men in Alaska or the States were suited to superintend the beginning reindeer industry. William Kjellmann, the one man fully qualified and interested, was twice called away to carry out other responsibilities connected with reindeer.

In the middle of 1895, Superintendent Kjellmann resigned to take his sick wife for treatment in the States. With them went their six-year-old daughter.

Kjellmann's assistant, J. C. Widstead, was appointed to take Kjellmann's place; Thorwald Kjellmann, father of William, became Widstead's assistant. Thorwald Kjellmann worked at the station, taking his turn

at herding, bringing in wood from the beach, fishing, and any other necessary work, until his death in May of 1898.

The winter of 1895-1896 was severe, resulting in a shortage of food in the villages surrounding Teller and short supplies at the station. T. L. Brevig's diary of the reindeer station activities indicates a lack of concern on Widstead's part for the welfare of the Eskimo herders.

In one instance, Brevig reported, Widstead had an opportunity to trade for new waterproof footwear for a herder, but did not. Instead he gave the herder badly worn mukluks that had been discarded. Killing of healthy reindeer still was not allowed because of the concentrated effort to build herds. Only the animals that died or that had to be killed because of injuries provided meat and skins.

Widstead was replaced by Kjellmann who returned to Alaska in 1896 without his family. Dr. A. N. Kittilsen, from Wisconsin, became Kjellmann's assistant.

Eaton Succeeds Teller

Kittilsen took charge of Teller while Kjellmann was away, traveling with the first Lapp trainers who were returning to their homeland and carrying out responsibilities to do with the Yukon reindeer expedition to help miners.

Because the reindeer moss had been pretty well consumed in the area surrounding Teller by 1897, a place on the Unalakleet River, about 300 miles to the east, was selected to become the main reindeer station. Dr. Kittilsen moved most of the herd there. The new station was named Eaton in honor of General John Eaton, past U.S. Commissioner of Education. Kittilsen's report for 1897-1898 gave a total of 446 adult deer and 177 fawns in the herd at Eaton.

With Brevig in charge, a small number of government reindeer were left at Teller to act as decoys for landing the deer brought from Siberia during the summer of 1898. A number of sled deer (steers) were also left at Teller. And three Eskimos stayed in the area with their deer: Tautook had earned 77 reindeer during his five years of apprenticeship, Sekeoglook had earned 59, and Wocksock owned 50.

When Kjellmann returned with the newcomers from Lapland he took charge at Eaton. He remained there until 1900, when he left due to sickness. In the interval, Dr. Kittilsen resigned to seek his fortune in the gold mines and Dr. Gambell, of Iowa, became the physician and assistant superintendent.

The reindeer at the new Eaton Station were centrally located for the new activity in Alaska. Herders from northern Norway, who arrived at the station in 1899, trained sled deer and pack deer for the use of the army as well as the miners, and delivered mail to the scattered mining camps and villages.

Meanwhile, Teller Reindeer Station closed in August of 1898, and so did the mission run by the Brevigs. No one could be found to keep Teller Mission open; Julia was in poor health, and the Brevigs needed a rest after four years of service in Alaska. Once back in the States, Brevig made reports on work in Alaska whenever he could and appealed for support for the mission at Teller.

During all the changes in the fledgling reindeer industry, the reindeer continued to multiply. More and more herds were established over a wide area.

Herders and their dog with a reindeer herd "corralled" by a burlap fence, all that's needed to hold the gentle deer. Courtesy of Glenbow Archives, Calgary, Alberta.

New Herds and Old

By 1899 herds existed from St. Michael to Point Barrow. The 1899 *Report* gives a total of 2,837 domestic reindeer in nine herds: 1,159 of these deer are reported as the personal property of 19 Eskimos who had learned the management of reindeer during five years' apprenticeship at the Government reindeer stations.[6]

Point Barrow now had 100 reindeer at the Presbyterian Mission. These deer, a portion of those driven north to help stranded whalers, had been kept as the nucleus of a herd for use as needed in future emergencies. Another 25 belonged to Oyello, an Eskimo apprentice. The remaining deer from the rescue drive were to go to Cape Prince of Wales or Teller Reindeer Station, except for 48 deer going to the mission station at Point Hope.

Point Hope had 100 head belonging to two Eskimo apprentices, Electoona and Ahlook; Teller had 300 belonging to the four Eskimos who stayed after the main reindeer station was moved to Eaton; and Golovin Bay had 209 at the Swedish Evangelical Mission plus 31 belonging to Eskimos. There were 209 at the Episcopal Mission at Tanana and another 52 belonging to the Eskimo, Moses. To replace the ones that had been borrowed from Antisarlook for the relief of the whalers, 328 were driven from Eaton to Point Rodney. This left 442 at Eaton. The Cape Prince of Wales herd of 714 belonged to the American Missionary Association under William Lopp and several Eskimo apprentices.

The yearly reports indicate that the arrival of fawns increased the size of herds more than an additional third every year. The females gave birth every year after they were a year old, and sometimes had twins. But it should be remembered that a number of reindeer wandered off with wild caribou when not carefully herded, were lost to predators and sickness, or were used for food. Also, deer in Alaska, like cattle in the States, were stolen.

Teller Properties Unprotected

While Eaton was busy with both administering reindeer activities and dealing with miners, the properties at Teller Reindeer Station were closed. Eskimos kept their reindeer in the vicinity, but did not use the buildings; the Brevigs had returned to the States on leave.

Sheldon Jackson had no funds to hire watchmen so he experimented with allowing a prospector to use a building through the winter of 1898-1899. In return, the miner agreed to care for the property, but he did not live up to his side of the agreement. The following winter the same arrangement was made on the recommendation of a Seattle business firm, allowing the use of one building while looking after the others. The man in charge was ignored by others, among them a U.S. deputy marshall.

Trespassers took over the main building and set up a saloon kept by an Eskimo woman. They wintered their dogs in one end of the building and occupied the other portion themselves. With no funds and no people available to reclaim the Teller properties, Jackson could do nothing for the time being.

11

Trials of Eskimos and Deer

The herding of reindeer offered Eskimos a continued connection with the natural environment that was the foundation of their culture. It was thought this would balance the changes required for reindeer herding. The biggest of the changes was the need to move the reindeer periodically to prevent overgrazing. This called for a less settled living than the hunting and fishing that Eskimos had known.

During winter it was necessary to find moss on the windswept higher areas. In the summer months, many herds were moved near the coast or rivers. The Eskimos would then catch fresh fish and other seafood. An added benefit was that both men and beasts could get a measure of relief from the swarms of mosquitos by getting into the water.

It cannot be said too often that it is hard to appreciate fully the complexity of establishing the reindeer industry for the Alaskan Eskimos—that, of necessity, the reindeer project in the American northland was experimental. White pioneers in Alaska education understood from the beginning that to become reindeer herders, Eskimos would need to change much of their way of life. Most people in the United States government did not seem to understand either the adaptive quality of Eskimo culture to the Alaskan environment or the extent of cultural changes required for reindeer herding.

No one could foresee the full effects whites would have on Eskimo culture. Nor could anyone foresee the deadly epidemics that some outsiders said were responsible for reducing the Eskimo population in villages along the Alaskan coast from thousands to hundreds.

Gold Claims and Reindeer Ranges

While reindeer became popular among miners, problems arose because of the mining activity. The influx of miners and traders near Nome disrupted the lives of Eskimo herders and their charges. Claims were staked regardless of grazing areas for herds. Violence erupted in and near villages that had increased in size practically overnight with the coming of gold hunters.

Most of the newcomers were honorable, hard-working men who saw the future possibilities of the reindeer industry. But enough men were thoughtless, or worse, to cause long-lasting damage.

Large areas of the moss range were destroyed when miners used fire to clear a claim—and left it to burn itself out. Others set the moss on fire just for the excitement of seeing it burn. The moss is slow-growing, at best, in this arctic region, taking ten to twenty years to replenish itself. The grazing habit of the reindeer, to nibble at the moss as it keeps moving along, fits this growth pattern. The vitality of the plant remains to nourish new growth. But the burning thoroughly destroyed the moss.

Epidemic

The first report of a life-threatening problem came to Sheldon Jackson when the cutter *Bear* returned from a deer-purchasing trip to Siberia in July 1899. Jackson learned of an epidemic among the people of the Siberian coast. The effort to bring more reindeer to Alaska was brought to a halt that year with only 29 animals purchased.

The Brevigs decided to return to Teller with Dagny and her newborn sister, Lenore, when an annual grant was given by the Lutheran church for the support of the mission. When the Brevigs reached Nome in July of 1900, the area was in a turmoil. Miners—by some accounts as many as 2,000—sifted the beach sands for gold. But more awful was the fact that two sailors, stricken with measles, had been put ashore at Nome by a whaling vessel. The disease was spreading.

Shocked, the Brevigs left as soon as possible for Teller Reindeer Station, hoping to avoid the measles infection, both for themselves and for the sake of those they would come in contact with at the reindeer station and mission. It was a two-day trip with dog team and sled. On reaching the station, they found the buildings had been vandalized. The miners who had taken advantage of the unprotected buildings had gone. The epidemic had already reached Teller.

The Brevigs set to work cleaning up. Soon Eskimos who had left the immediate area around the station when the miners came began to trickle back. They wanted to come near, but first always asked to make sure that no other white men besides the station people were around.

Eskimos reported to the Brevigs that many in their families were sick or had died. At Cape Prince of Wales, almost all of the population was infected, and called for help. The lack of medicine and other supplies and equipment, as well as of food, made the situation seem almost hopeless. But the Brevigs did the best they could.

This was at the beginning of an epidemic of flu, pneumonia, and measles that swept the Asiatic side of the Bering Sea, the Aleutian Islands, the Seward Peninsula, the Arctic, and the lower Yukon River.

Reverend Brevig with his wife and daughter. Photograph by Larson in the 1899 *Report on Introduction of Domestic Reindeer into Alaska.*

The letters of T. L. Brevig from Teller Mission provide a sad, but clear picture of the effects of the epidemic in the surrounding area and the growing hunger of survivors. There were more sick people than well. Many were so weakened that they could not catch and dry fish to store for the coming winter. Brevig wrote to both Captain Jarvis of the Revenue Cutter Service and Sheldon Jackson, seeking food supplies.

In spite of the epidemic and all the problems it brought, people like the Brevigs stayed on and continued their work. Brevig mentions in one letter that with all the sickness they had not been able to hold classes regularly, but evening school was still held at times.

Before the year 1901 passed, half the Eskimo population died in the Teller Station area alone; the situation was not much better in many other areas. The number of children without families grew as the epidemic moved through the villages.

The Brevigs began to take in orphans. A station building was repaired at the expense of the Brevigs' church to provide shelter. That was the beginning of Teller Orphanage, later known as Brevig Orphanage. One of the first orphans was a foundling who later became a strong advocate for her people.

Child in Snowdrift

A prospector, pulling his sled loaded with supplies, was startled by the whimpers of a child in the snowdrift. He found the nearly-frozen little girl, about two years old, very near death. He wrapped her in furs and hurried along to the mission at Teller Reindeer Station and turned her over to Julia Brevig.

The little girl was named Emma, after the daughter of the man who sent a box of baby clothing to the mission. Emma was later told that it took her three years to thaw out. Before that she just wouldn't talk, and didn't

want to be with people. Then, all of a sudden, she just opened up. "It was as if all I wanted to do was catch up."[7]

Under the care of Julia Brevig, Emma thrived. She learned to speak Norwegian, the mother tongue of the Brevigs, as well as English and her native Eskimo language. Her eyes had been so badly damaged by freezing that reading was a problem. But by using raised letters on blocks Emma was able to keep up with the other children.

Emma's training was in a religious environment, but it was also practical. She learned the household skills of the "outside" world, but also was fully equipped to live in her own Eskimo world. This was a priority as the Brevigs helped the many orphans in their care. Emma helped drag in ice blocks for drinking water along three miles of beach. She hauled driftwood across miles of ice and snow. She baked tubs of bread. She prepared natural foods in the way of Eskimo custom.

When she became of school age, Emma attended the government school with the other children, seven miles across the bay from the mission:

Before a teacher came to reside at the mission, we went to school at Teller town. Papa Brevig made knots and loops in a long rope to which we clung on the way across the ice and snow to school, so we would not become separated. At times it seems my arms and hands still ache from the strain of pulling at that rope. We learned early to help each other.[8]

Tending the Reindeer Herds

The epidemic took many of the promising apprentices as well as owners of small herds. Most of the Eskimos who survived the winter of 1900-1901 were too weak or too young to tend the reindeer herds.

As many Lapps as were available and willing to help with the herding were re-hired. A number of Lapps were so successful at the placer mines that Jackson had to increase salaries substantially to keep any of them with the reindeer.

In cases where Eskimo relatives took over herds, they followed their own cultural rules of inheritance. Mary Antisarlook, along with her husband's two brothers, took over the herd when Charley died in 1900.

No government rules had been established for inheritance. Some white men took advantage of the situation, and married Eskimo widows who had taken over their late husbands' herds. When, in later years, nonnatives involved themselves in reindeer herds

---

Emma Willoya

The child found in a snowdrift during the epidemics of 1899-1901 grew into a woman. Her life spanned the first fifty years of the reindeer industry in Alaska and beyond. As a woman raising a large family during many years of extreme hardship, Emma experienced firsthand the clashes between the culture of her people and government administration. An Eskimo of great determination, Emma often spoke out for her people. (Much of what follows is information gleaned from recordings Emma made of her memories.)

At about 17 Emma married David Willoya, a reindeer herder who earlier had attended classes at Teller Mission. He had started herding his uncle's reindeer at the age of twelve. He became an expert in caring for reindeer and was often called on to help other owners. The uncle had a large herd and when he died of tuberculosis his herd became David Willoya's because David had cared for it.

After marrying David, Emma took her turn at regular eight-hour shifts with the herd. In a year she earned her first deer. In time she had a special, very tame sled deer that she was particularly fond of. She recalled curling up against Whitey's warm body while out tending the herd.

The Willoyas tended their herd in the traditional way, living at their reindeer camp so they could watch their animals closely. They trapped furs and fished to help support their growing family. They had six children.

David was injured while training a sled deer. An antler thrust deeply into his chest, and removing it left an ugly wound that was slow in healing.

He later died of smallpox.

An ongoing discussion among the Eskimo herders concerned the "homing instinct" of reindeer. Emma's view that Whitey, her favorite sled deer, would return—from anywhere—once he was turned loose was put to the test. Mr. Shields, the superintendent of the government herds at that time, borrowed Emma's pet deer for his inspection trip to Point Barrow. One year—two years passed. Then, one morning, Whitey stuck his head into Emma's tent door. Almost three years it had taken Whitey to find his way over trackless mountains and tundra to get back to Teller from where he was turned loose, about ten miles out of Point Barrow.

Emma moved with her reindeer herd to the settlement of Cripple Creek, where an epidemic had left 17 children parentless. There she cared for the motherless children of Mike, her late husband's brother. Later she and Mike were married and had six children.

During the years of World War II there were 11,000 troops stationed in the Nome area. Some servicemen used the reindeer for target practice. They showed such disrespect for the Eskimos who tried to stop them that Emma decided to stand up to them. Going with her dogteam and sled to where the men were aiming at the reindeer, she lowered her parka hood to show them she was a woman, and explained how they were destroying animals that belonged to someone—that they were needed to feed the families.

After the flu epidemic of 1918, when so many

Emma Willoya (*continued*)

reindeer herders died, Emma was one of many survivors whose deer were incorporated in a reindeer association. Under the rules of the association no one was allowed to reclaim marked deer, even to feed a hungry family. Emma saw government men put as many as a dozen at a time in jail for trying to butcher their own deer to feed their families.

Soon Emma and her family moved again, some 12 miles out of Nome, the "Gold City." A new law said that all children had to attend school, and Nome had the only school in the area. With her deer gone, Emma had a hard time feeding her family. As soon as school was out on Fridays, she took her children to camp on the tundra where they could catch ptarmigan and rabbits. This way she "built them up" so they could survive for the school week in town.

A determined person, Emma managed to provide for her immediate family—and at the same time to provide for her people an important link between two very different cultures. Her language skills were invaluable. One day she would interpret for a surgeon at the hospital, another day for a judge in court. Emma's knowledge of languages was at times a surprise and a delight. In 1926 she dumbfounded Roald Amundsen, the Norwegian explorer, who had completed his first flight over the North Pole in the dirigible *Norge*. She greeted him in Nome by singing his national anthem in fluent Norwegian.

When her children were grown, Emma became increasingly active in mission work. She moved into Nome in 1946, where she could be more helpful in matters that concerned Natives in general. She was a member of the Native school board and secretary of the Nome Eskimo community. While she was on the school board, she was asked "What would be the best practical help for young Native girls?" She answered, "To learn to sew." So she found herself working with the Native Skin Sewers' Cooperative, which she headed for almost 16 years.

During and after the war years Emma and her team of skilled sewers made thousands of warm skin garments for the servicemen stationed in the far north. A letter of thanks from President Harry Truman "for selfless service in your country's time of need" became a prized possession.

Although her eyes never fully healed from the freezing as an infant, Emma regained considerable sight by 1960. Then, in 1971, she had a stroke that left her completely blind. Still, her sharp mind and keen memory made her a valuable spokesperson for the Native community. She was always particularly vocal about the reindeer activities in which she took part all her life.

She saw Alaska become the 49th state on January 3, 1959. She frequently spoke for her people during the long struggle that led to passage of the Alaska Native Claims Settlement Act in 1971, which secured Native rights to village sites and traditional ways of life.

In 1972 Emma appeared before Alaska Senators Mike Gravel and Ted Stevens at a hearing on legislation to protect marine mammals. Although completely blind and physically frail, she still had a clear, firm voice: "What are we going to do if hunting rights are taken away from us? Others may kill for profit or sport, but for us the hunting of sea mammals is a matter of existence." An exemption was included in the 1972 Marine Mammal Protection Act allowing Alaska's indigenous people to continue to hunt sea animals for food and clothing, although not for commercial purposes.

Church was important to Emma. There was no Lutheran congregation when she and her family moved to Nome, so they joined the Methodist church. When a Lutheran congregation was established in 1959, she returned to the roots of her Christian faith, where she worked in many leadership positions. When her health began to fail in 1982 she moved to a hospital in Anchorage. After a lifetime of service to her people, Emma died February 27, 1983.

Teller Reindeer Station in Winter   (Eskimo Drawing)

Courtesy of National Archives.

for commercial profit, the questions of inheritance and ownership arose again.

At the time, the problem of ownership was less important to the leaders of the reindeer project than making sure that as many as possible of the reindeer were tended. This was crucial if the reindeer industry was to continue after this epidemic had passed.

Besides the loss of herders, another real threat to the future of the reindeer came from the dogs that ran wild. The large number of Eskimo families that died during the

epidemic released their dogs from all ownership and controls. With no one to feed them, the dogs had to find food for themselves. In former days they hunted caribou, so they naturally attacked the reindeer at every opportunity. Many of the dogs had to be shot.

The usually hardy Eskimos suffered greatly from the loss of family members to diseases that were even more frightening because previously unknown. Those living in the northland were relieved when the epidemic at last ended.

12

The First Fifteen Years

The fifteenth anniversary of the birth of the domestic reindeer industry in Alaska could have been a time for celebration. The project to establish herds among the Eskimo villages as quickly as possible, and to teach basic language and record keeping in the industrial schools had come a long way since 1890.

Jackson and others who actually experienced conditions in Alaska dealt as best they could with a variety of problems, including communication over vast uncharted tundra. Another difficulty was securing construction labor and teachers, and providing them with supplies, particularly north of the Aleutians. The arrival of only one freight ship a year, with the delivery of its load dependent on weather and ice conditions, made living conditions primitive by standards in towns and cities in the States.

Even with willing hands, construction of school buildings and living quarters was slowed by the long winters and short summers. Building materials often arrived so late in the season that construction had to wait until winter gave way to another summer.

In the face of these difficulties, much had been accomplished. Whites and Eskimos involved in the reindeer project worked together to build the reindeer industry.

By late in 1902, when the Russian government ended exportation of reindeer to Alaska, a total of 1,280 had been brought to the Seward Peninsula. Loans of reindeer from government herds continued throughout northwestern and northern Alaska. By 1904 there were ten stations: Point Barrow, Kotzebue, Cape Prince of Wales, St. Lawrence Island, Teller, Golovin, Unalakleet, Eaton, Nulato, and Bethel. The herds were owned by the government, missions, and individual Eskimos, Lapps, and Finns.

Standard Schools

Those who attended school were not only the younger children, but adults as well. They saw the need to read and write English as well as speak it. But when the word was passed that walrus—or seal, or beluga, or bowhead whale—had been sighted, the entire village stopped all other activities to concentrate on that food supply. This was the time for harvest—to lay up food for the bleak days ahead.

The success of the teacher depended on an understanding of the subsistence life style of the community. A teacher quickly learned that this was also a part of surviving and that what affected one member in the village affected all. Daily diaries kept through the years by the teachers and superintendents reveal the day-to-day activities at the stations, schools, and missions.

Industrial Schools and Hospitals

In the 1904 *Report* on reindeer in Alaska, Jackson emphasized benefits of the reindeer project to both whites and Eskimos. In many ways a highly practical man, perhaps he thought this emphasis might help to assure the availability of funds to continue helping the Eskimos build the reindeer industry.

In support of Alaskan schools and the reindeer industry, Jackson recalled President Theodore Roosevelt's recent message to Congress. Roosevelt had called attention to, in Jackson's words, "the changed conditions which have come to the natives of Alaska with the advent of large numbers of white men in their country" and "their need of attention, especially in the way of industrial schools and hospitals."[9]

Concerning industrial schools, Jackson reported that Eskimos had proven their ability to use reindeer for carrying mail, freight, and passengers. He stated that reindeer herding and teaming could provide cheap food and transportation for immigrants, thus benefiting both Eskimos and whites.

Although some of Jackson's arguments may look as if they favor white immigrants to Alaska, what he advocated would support Eskimos in maintaining as much autonomy as possible in the midst of the growing white population. His recommendations included increasing the number of small industrial schools and placing of the schools so as to be convenient to Alaskan native populations.

Concerning hospitals, Jackson noted the Secretary of Interior's repeated calls to Congress for hospitals in Alaska. Jackson saw that because of the lack of communication of any kind between the scattered settlements, a hospital would serve a very limited area. When establishing stations/schools, Jackson made sure that a physician was in residence. Upon occasion he employed a doctor to be teacher and/or reindeer superintendent at a station.

Reindeer, which can dig through deep snow to find the lichen (moss) on which they thrive, are well suited to Alaska's long winter. Courtesy of Alaska Historical Library, Juneau.

In initially establishing the industrial schools Jackson contacted the various missions that had already gathered a number of native families about them. He was aware of the confusion that might be caused by introducing another religious faith into a community; his practice was to honor the church that was already at home in the area. More than once he contacted the head of that church to advise and seek further help for its mission in Alaska. From these activities it is clear that Jackson was ecumenical way ahead of his time.

The reindeer were the magnet to bring Eskimos into the classroom to learn the elements of reading, writing, record keeping, and speaking English—the natural subject to emphasize because Eskimos would need to know English to communicate and do business with white people in coming years. Drawing, sewing, and housework were also taught. Girls already learned skin sewing at an early age. Now they had white man's yard goods to fashion into garments.

Apprentice Training

Jackson's 1904 *Report* recounts the training requirements of an apprentice. For five years the young men were placed in an industrial branch of the public school system to learn about the raising, care, and management of reindeer. Skilled Finn or Lapp reindeer men were their instructors. During this training the apprentice earned his room and board. He was supported by the mission, the government, or the herder, depending upon his location.

The *Report on the Introduction of Domestic Reindeer into Alaska* for 1904 shows 2,774 reindeer at ten stations and lists over 60 reindeer owners and apprentices.

Herders and Their Reindeer

Point Barrow

Ahlook	185
Shoudla	70
Toktuk and Panigeo	55
Segevan	45
Paneoneo	37
Powyun	34
Ungawishak	30
Ingnoven	13

Kotzebue (Arctic)

Electoona	158
Otpelle	34
Okomon	7
Oghoalook	7
Minungon	8
Munnok	5

Wales

George Ootenna	98
Thomas Sokwena	50
James Keok	88
S. Kivyeargruk	93
Jos. Enungwouk	24
Frank Iyatunguk	21
Peter Ibiono	7
Ohbook	7
Eraheruk	1

Gambell (St Lawrence Is)

Putlkinhok	27
Sepillu	20
Penin (or Pinink)	9
Oonmookok	2

Teller

Albikok (or Allikok)	191
Dannak (or Dunnak)	72
Sekeoglook	75
Serawlook	7
Carrook	6

Golofnin (or Golovin)

Tautook	172
Constantine	43
Taktuk	39
Ahmahktoolik	19
John	10
Albert	7
Benjamin	6
Peter	6
Mrs. Dexter	8

Unalakleet

Okitkon	97
Tatpan	138
Stephan Ivanoff	48
Bikongan	4
Moses Koutchok	5

Eaton

Nallogoroak	63
Mary Andrewuk	358
Koktoak (or Kotoak)	46
Angolook	58
Sagoonuk	49
Acebuk	27
Avogook	17
Amikravinik	17
Frank Kauchak	5
Sakpillok	5

Bethel (Kuskokwim)

Waseby	15
Robert	16
Tommy	5
Henry	5

Nulato

number of deer unknown

Stephen Annu
Alexander Kulana
John Rorondelel

Reindeer milling in ice corral at Wainwright. Courtesy of University of Oregon, Special Collections, Knight Library (C. L. Andrews Collection).

In addition to a basic living, an apprentice earned two female deer each year—on a loan basis. The offspring became his personal property, with his own earmark, but subject to government control over slaughter and sale. By the end of five years, the offspring from ten females would constitute a substantial beginning for a private herd. The size of his herd would depend on the aptitude of the apprentice, and his attentiveness.

The animals would continue under the supervision of the government for 20 years. This seems restrictive, but given the cultural changes that were taking place, this was an obvious precaution and protection for the new herd owner. The elders were accustomed to helping themselves to any food gotten by a family member: that was the cultural pattern. It was thought that it would take two or three more generations to understand the new pattern of independence of children to meet the challenge of the future.

Planning for Chains of Stations

In the early years of using sled deer for various purposes it became clear that relay stations, or a chain of stations, would be necessary. It was customary for dog teams to be replaced with fresh dogs during the course of any lengthy travel. The reindeer did not have to carry their food, but they required frequent stops for resting and grazing.

Jackson planned to establish chains of reindeer stations to facilitate travel by traders, miners, the army, and others. The first important line of travel was from Cape Prince of Wales east along the northern coast of the Bering Sea to Unalakleet, 350 miles; the second from Cape Prince of Wales north along the Arctic Ocean to Barrow, 850 miles. A map that Jackson had prepared for the 1904 *Report* shows stations and the dates they were established, and also indicates proposed future locations.

Counting the Reindeer

Reindeer counts were made twice a year after rounding up the reindeer into corrals. Spring roundups were held soon after fawning time, to take a count of the females and fawns. This was also the best time to mark fawns with their mothers' earmarks because they followed their mothers closely. Most of the male fawns were castrated at this time, saving out only the strongest for breeding purposes. Some of the older steers would be separated out for training to harness and sled work. Another roundup and count of the reindeer occurred in the fall, at which time some of the animals were slaughtered for food and clothing.

Roundups were exciting times for all the families involved. Entire households moved to the corral area. The children enjoyed playtime on the tundra, while the adults cooperated in the work at hand. To handle and count 200 or 300 and up to 1,500 animals was a large task, and the community gathering sometimes lasted for several days.

Keeping Track of Funds

In the years 1894 to 1905, Congress appropriated a total of $207,500 for the domestic reindeer industry in Alaska. Jackson kept an account of the reindeer funds spent each year, listing cost of reindeer; building materials for living quarters of herders, teachers, and superintendents; salaries, supplies, freight, and

Roundups

The fall roundups at Wainwright were described by Clarence L. Andrews. They were usually held in October, after the marshes and lakes were frozen into smooth pavements. The Eskimos would scour the tundra with their reindeer teams to gather the antlered wanderers close to the village.

Choosing a nearby lake, the Eskimos watched for the ice to get ten to twelve inches thick. Then squads of men would go out with ice saws and big ice tongs and cut blocks about six feet long and two feet wide. These blocks were dragged out and hauled to the place selected for the corral.

To build the corral, the blocks were set on end then a little water was poured around the bottoms to settle them into place and freeze them to the ground. Hour after hour the work would go on until an oval ice wall was formed that was about 200 feet wide and 300 feet long, with a lead to the entrance and a chute at both ends.

Into the corral they drove the reindeer—a thousand or more—as quietly as possible. Frightened because they had not been confined in a corral for a whole year, the animals would trot round and round the wall, with mouths open, breath steaming in the cold air, hooves clacking. A rope closed the entrance, and two or three boys or girls stood guard to prevent any escape.

At the exit several deer at a time were cut out of the herd and put through the funnel-shaped chute. A checker recorded the owner's mark, the sex, and whether the deer was fawn or adult. If a deer came into the chute without a mark, it would be caught and a sharp blade or emasculator would quickly do its work. Then the ear-marked reindeer would be freed to join others on the tundra.

During the later years—late 20s and into the 30s—the spring roundups were considered an unnecessary expense, and they were no longer held. This delay in marking made the fall roundup doubly difficult and complicated. Ownership of the so-called strays would be hard to identify, as the older fawns would no longer be attached to their mothers. This was one of the problems that continued to complicate matters as the years passed.

rations for Lapps; and traveling expenses for Jackson or his assistant, William Hamilton.

Considering the size of the area, the scattered inhabitants that were served, and the necessity of trial and error in developing a totally new industry in Alaska, the reindeer statistics for the years from 1892 to 1905 are impressive.

The tables that Jackson prepared for the annual *Reports* give an idea of how quickly the reindeer multiplied. Because counting reindeer was not easy—and counting reindeer was not a task that the people involved in the project were used to—the specific numbers may not be completely accurate. But the absolute numbers are not so important as what is clear from comparing the numbers year to year: reindeer in Alaska increased more than sevenfold from 1892 to 1905. From 1,280 reindeer imported from Siberia, the deer in Alaska multiplied to more than 10,000 despite the various problems already described.

Tables in each *Report* give an idea, too, of the success of the apprenticeship program. By 1904, at least 60 Eskimos owned more than 2,700 deer. Nearly all had served five years of apprenticeship. Another 61 Eskimos were in training to become herders, but owned no deer as yet. Under the charge of the graduates more reindeer stations opened as links in the proposed chain of stations for the mail routes in Arctic Alaska.

Fifteen reindeer stations opened during the period from 1892 to 1905. From the original station at Teller, eight stations received reindeer, and reindeer husbandry got under way as far north as Barrow and as far to the south as Iliamna, on Cook Inlet. The move of the major part of the government herd to Eaton came in 1898. The hectic first years at Eaton, with all the mining and military needs, saw much reindeer activity, but left little opportunity to establish new stations. But in 1905 five new stations opened, at Kivalina, Deering, Iliamna, Bettles, and Shishmaref.

This expanse of territory called for the appointment of regional superintendents. So in 1905 Dr. C. O. Lund was made superintendent of the central region: Golovin Bay area, Norton Sound, and the valleys of the Yukon and Kuskokwim rivers. The Northwest District, as it was called, was along the shores of the Bering Sea and the Arctic Ocean. William Lopp, whose involvement in the reindeer industry began in 1894, was placed in charge of both the reindeer herds and the schools in this district.

Eskimo school girl with cooking utensils. Photograph by J. W. Kelly in the 1894 *Report on Introduction of Domestic Reindeer Into Alaska.*

13

Different Viewpoints

What could have been a celebration of the accomplishments of the reindeer project up to 1905 turned into arguments among government officials in Washington. While the reindeer went on increasing and more stations were built in Alaska, discussion continued in Washington over the merits of reindeer and education in the northland. Some people had opposed the entire reindeer project from the beginning. Not everyone was satisfied with the progress of the education program as they learned of it from informal and formal reports.

Newcomers

People who questioned whether reindeer activities and education were too closely connected with the various missions did not seem to take into account that few people were willing to face the living conditions in "Seward's Folly" and become government teachers to the people of that land.

The new territory beckoned the pioneer and the adventurer seeking personal gain. Missionaries came to spread Christianity, and felt compelled to try to rectify the extensive damage done to the land and people, and through education to help them cope with the encroaching white man's world. Some people came as government teachers.

Churchill's Report

In 1905 the annual inspection of schools and reindeer was made by William Hamilton, Jackson's assistant, who had covered the tour of Alaska in earlier seasons when he was needed. Sheldon Jackson was not well enough to make the rigorous trip. He remained in his Washington, D.C., office and prepared a comprehensive review of the Alaskan program to date.

In the same year, the Department of the Interior sent Frank C. Churchill to investigate the Alaskan school system and the reindeer industry. Churchill resigned his position as an inspector with the Indian Service to travel to Alaska.

Sailing from Seattle, Washington, on June 14, 1905 on his new assignment, Churchill reached Nome, Alaska, on July 3. There he joined the revenue cutter *Thetis* on its regular annual cruise. The ship took him first to Gambell on St. Lawrence Island, then east and north to Golovin, Teller, Wales, and Deering, and along the Arctic coast to Point Barrow. From there the *Thetis* went back south to Nome, again east to Gambell, then south through the Aleutian chain into the north Pacific Ocean and down to southeastern Alaska. Churchill departed for Seattle, Washington, on October 5 from Ketchikan.

By the nature of this kind of tour, much

of Churchill's time was spent traveling on the ship. Churchill said in his report that there was too little time to accomplish all that he was sent to do. Nonetheless, the report he submitted to Congress was critical of Jackson's work in Alaska: as a missionary, as administrator of the newly established school system, as organizer of the reindeer industry.

The report shows that Churchill believed that Jackson was operating under a conflict of interest with the funds Congress was providing him as the Agent of Education while he was also receiving funds as a missionary for the Presbyterian church. The implication was that Jackson was more interested in bringing native people to his faith than with training them as citizens. Churchill also stated his belief that it would be best if Eskimos had full control of the reindeer they earned. He further reported that schools were poorly attended.

A Matter of Opinion

The Churchill report drew angry criticism from many who were involved with the schools and the reindeer in Alaska. It was seen as an example of how difficult it was for people who had experienced the northland only briefly to understand what Jackson and others were trying to accomplish, and the difficulties that arose again and again in establishing and strengthening the reindeer industry for Eskimos. For instance, according to some letter writers, Churchill seemed to have no concept of the difficulty imposed by climate in getting supplies to build schools. And in reporting on school attendance he did not take into consideration that during the time he was in Alaska it was the season to set up camps for gathering fish and seal, and preparing them for winter storage.

When the Government Printing Office published Jackson's final *Report* in 1908, many letters were reprinted explaining how people in Alaska viewed Churchill's visit and his report.

Brevig, who had been involved with the reindeer and schools from the beginning, wrote of many inconsistencies in Churchill's report. In fact, Brevig listed errors in the report that indicated lack of knowledge of distances between stations and a lack of understanding of the apprenticeship program.

The missionary of the Society of Friends at Kotzebue, Dana Thomas, described Churchill's visit:

Although Kotzebue contained a public school in session and had an important reindeer herd, Mr. Churchill did not deem it of sufficient importance to visit. Captain Hamlet, of the Thetis, *William Hamilton, Mr. Lopp, and Judge Landers, of Nome, came ashore from the revenue cutter. I inquired for Mr. Churchill and was told he was too busy trading for a mastodon "tusk" to come ashore.* [10]

The teacher/reindeer superintendent on St. Lawrence Island, E. O. Campbell, wrote that Mr. Churchill spent less than a total of 15 minutes in conversation with him during his two stops at the island. Campbell also wrote that one of the oldest and most intelligent apprentices, Sepillu, who had made the trip with Churchill to Point Barrow and back on the *Thetis*, was asked no questions by Churchill. This in spite of the fact that Sepillu had completed his five years' apprenticeship and could speak English fairly well.

Supporters of the reindeer project as administered by Jackson also felt that Churchill did not understand the principles of loans to the missions. A loan of 100 animals was made to a mission for a period of five years, with the understanding that at the end of that time the mission would return 100 to the government, and retain the increase from the loaned herd. Jackson expected that the mission would use any surplus steers for food and clothing or as sled deer, and would continue training apprentices. For the duration of their apprenticeship, the Eskimos were expected to keep the deer they earned with the mission herd.

The concern of people like Churchill that natives should own reindeer outright did not take into account one of the important reasons for the apprenticeship program. This program was not only to assure adequate training in reindeer husbandry, but to ensure careful management of the deer during the time that social and cultural adjustments were occurring at all age and social levels. It was believed that these adjustments would take considerable time.

Evidence of Dissent

Changes were introduced as a result of Churchill's report. In fact, his investigation and report represent a turning point in government policy toward Alaskan schools and the reindeer industry.

When Congress appropriated additional funds for reindeer stations and for instruction of Alaskan natives in reindeer herding in 1906, provisions of the act appeared to ignore Churchill's view that mission involvement in the reindeer industry should stop. At least

Lomen and Company men marking a herd and castrating males at Kotzebue, Alaska, 1915. Courtesy of Glenbow Archives, Calgary, Alberta.

Little Eskimo child and reindeer. Courtesy of Glenbow Archives, Calgary, Alberta.

the opinion of one lawyer for the government suggests that the original plans for a reindeer industry were still thought the best by a majority in Congress.

Frank L. Campbell, an assistant attorney general, responded to a request for an opinion on the new act passed by Congress in 1906. He was asked whether the Secretary of the Interior, under one of the provisions in the act, could turn over a number of reindeer to Alaskan natives. This particular provision said that Congress was making funds available for the support of reindeer stations in Alaska, and for the instruction of Alaskan natives in the care and management of the reindeer. The provision further directed that all reindeer owned by the government should be turned over to the missions in Alaska as soon as was practical. The missions would hold and use the deer according to conditions

set by the Secretary of the Interior. In Campbell's opinion:

There would not seem to be room for difference of opinion as to the meaning of this statute. It in plain terms directs that all reindeer owned by the United States in Alaska shall be turned over to the Alaskan missions, and nowhere provides that the natives shall have any part or parcel thereof. . . .

A report by Frank C. Churchill . . . tends to show that the holding of reindeer by missions in Alaska is not for the best interests of the natives, but this is a question of policy which the Congress of the United States in the rightful exercise of its powers has determined adversely to said report and presumably after a full investigation of the subject.

I advise you that there is no authority in said act for turning over any Alaskan reindeer to the natives, but suggest that the Secretary of the Interior may prescribe such conditions to the mission use of this property as may contribute to the best interests of the natives. The act in question clearly contemplates this, and I am inclined to the belief that it was thought better results could be secured for the natives in this way than by intrusting them with the management of the property. [11]

In short, Campbell thought Congress intended that the government would stop holding herds, but the missions would continue with herds and the training of Eskimos in reindeer husbandry.

The years that followed the 1906 act and Churchill's investigation were no less turbulent than the years before. Basic disagreements in Washington did not help to clarify matters for those working in Alaska—either Eskimos or whites. Furthermore, living conditions in Alaska for both man and beast kept changing rapidly as more people came north to engage in mining and other businesses.

14

A New Era in the Reindeer Industry

The reindeer project was less than twenty years old in 1907. Contact with white people—scoundrels and friends alike—had inevitably led to weakening, and at times breaking, of Eskimo cultural patterns. Herding required much time and apprentices frequently depended on the white people who managed the deer to provide them food and shelter. For these Eskimo pioneers, the ways of the hunter largely had to be set aside.

Social antagonism occurred. The first apprentices were often scorned for abandoning the old ways, particularly by fathers who were accustomed to teaching their sons. Parents could not understand the new independence of their male offspring. Nor could they see why they were not supposed to take reindeer if they wanted to: it had always been

Alfred Nilima, a Lapp herd owner, and one of his reindeer. Courtesy of Glenbow Archives, Calgary, Alberta.

their right according to the Eskimo way.

But the change from purely Eskimo ways to a new way of life was under way. Indeed, hard feelings about reindeer herding were easing within Eskimo families and villages. As the second generation came along, once again father could teach son.

Still, as Eskimo reindeer herds became established, other problems arose. By Eskimo custom the reindeer belonging to the father would pass to the son(s); by U.S. law the wife inherited the deer. This important difference in cultural patterns led to bad feelings among Eskimos.

Also, Eskimos disliked the federal rules that continued government oversight of reindeer belonging to natives. The federal government had ruled in the beginning of the industry that no live female deer could be sold by natives. Sales were limited to steers, whether for meat or for sled deer.

Non-native ownership of reindeer became a larger issue. The number of reindeer in non-native herds increased, and questions about range grew more urgent for Eskimos. Non-native reindeer owners made their own rules about disposing of the animals they owned as they saw fit. This difference in treatment was hard for Eskimos to take.

More Rules and Regulations

Harlan Updegraff, Chief of the Alaska Division, Bureau of Education, made the annual inspection trips for the bureau in 1907 and 1908. His report of 1908 describes his recommendations for public schools and how distribution of reindeer herds was progressing.

Updegraff stressed the necessity of granting to the native peoples of Alaska the same rights and privileges under the public land mineral laws as those enjoyed by citizens of the United States. His report made plain the abuses of white men toward the unsuspecting natives in most of their social and business dealings. He urged the Secretary of the Interior to establish authorities to protect the native people and assist them in establishing their own industries, to establish sanitary codes and health care, to require school attendance, to outlaw sale of intoxicants to natives, and to provide sufficient funds for their education. He emphasized that an addition to earlier rules should allow Eskimos to receive deer instead of cash when they were being paid for labor in connection with government services.

The thrust of Updegraff's recommendations about the reindeer industry and the consequent rules and regulations passed by Congress were aimed at developing more rapid distribution of the reindeer among the native peoples. The intent was to remove the reindeer from government, missions, and Lapps so that the increase of the herds would belong to the native Alaskan people, and it would be truly a native industry.

To start with, Updegraff said, large numbers of government-owned reindeer should be transferred to Eskimos and other native peoples wherever they had an interested, trained herder/owner. He was particularly concerned that new herds should be established in remote villages where he observed the threat of starvation. He also recognized the need for supervision that would establish widely spread herds, with sufficient apprentices to absorb the sizable annual herd increase and establish new herds.

These appeared to be good long-range goals. However, only the government herds were affected by the rules laid down. The mission-owned herds, and those of the Lapps, continued to increase. In fact, there were Lapps who had visions of developing extensive herds comparable to those in their homeland—an indication of success and wealth. Non-natives continued to develop their herds in commercial dimensions in open conflict with native interests and government policies.

Loading frozen reindeer carcasses to take to market. Courtesy of Glenbow Archives, Calgary, Alberta.

Electoona, Okpolick, Seveck, Onalick

While disagreements continued among Eskimos and whites about what reindeer policy should be, practical people were getting on with the matter of raising reindeer. One of the most successful Eskimo herds had begun in the winter of 1904-1905. Two graduate apprentices, Electoona and Okpolick, moved their earned animals to Kivalina, a village southeast of Point Hope. Their combined herd totaled 220.

In 1908 the government sent 200 additional reindeer to join this herd. To help with the herding, the government also added two more apprentices, Chester Seveck and George Onalick.

Seveck and Onalick were both 18 years old. Each was paid, in addition to food and supplies, six live reindeer the first year, eight the second year, ten the third, and ten the fourth. They then became graduate herders. By 1912 Seveck separated his earned deer

and their offspring, and formed another herd with Electoona's deer.

The experience of these Eskimos showed that upwards of twenty years of apprenticeship was not always necessary—at least not to learn good herding practices.

A Surplus of Reindeer

The local superintendents of the Bureau of Education—who were the village school teachers—had no difficulty in placing reindeer in the hands of native learners. The increase of herds and of herd owners brought more problems. Those who were better learners and managers naturally developed larger herds and became highly respected— even envied—to the point of creating a "reindeer aristocracy" for a few years.

The success in increasing the herds both in number and in size soon meant the local markets were flooded. In 1909 arrangements

Chester Asakak Seveck

In his autobiography, *Longest Reindeer Herder*, Chester Seveck says he was born in the winter of 1890 at a camping ground on the Kivalina River, and first attended school there at what became the village of Kivalina. He learned the life of subsistence from his father, who was a successful hunter and whaler. Then in 1908 he became a government apprentice herder, working with the herd begun at Kivalina in 1905 by Electoona and Okpolick. By the time five years had passed, Seveck was an established herder/owner. For the next 46 years he was a reindeer herder and manager.

In his youth Chester survived for ten days on floating ice that had broken away from shore. He had caught a seal, but it was too heavy to drag along so his only food was a rawhide rope. The only way he had of getting water was to scrape away the top of the salty ice and chip at a lower layer. His parents thought they were seeing a ghost when he finally staggered home.

When he and Tillie Ferriera married in 1912 they immediately set up housekeeping at the Point Hope reindeer camp. In the same year Seveck took Reindeer Superintendent Walter Shields to Point Barrow. He used six trained sled deer pulling four sleds. Their equipment included tent, camp stove, primus stove, sleeping bags, and good warm clothes.

On the way to Barrow a violent blizzard struck and three deer disappeared. After waiting out the storm for three days, Chester found the lost deer and they continued on to Barrow. After staying there for two weeks they began the return trip. When they were met by a messenger who told him his wife was having their first child, Seveck borrowed a dog team and rushed to his wife. This was

were made with the Department of Agriculture to export reindeer meat, hides, and antlers through the Bureau of Education. In the fall of 1911, 125 carcasses were shipped to Seattle from Nome, the first sale and export of reindeer meat by Eskimo herders. However, no long-range provisions were made by the Bureau of Education for exporting reindeer products. This was the opportunity for non-native interests to step into the production line and establish a marketing system.

Lomen Enterprise

In 1900, when Gudbrand Lomen's son Carl decided to go to Nome to search for gold, the father decided to take a vacation and travel with him. Upon arriving in Nome that summer, Gudbrand and Carl learned that the tents of those panning for gold stretched for miles in all directions. Gudbrand, an attorney, found himself busy immediately, dealing with mining claims and disputes.

As winter approached, the family at home wanted Carl and his father to return. But the law practice was so pressing that the elder Lomen could not leave, and Carl was enjoying the life of a sourdough. It was three years before they returned home. And then it was because Carl came down with typhoid fever.

After recovering and resting at home, Carl was aboard the first steamer leaving Seattle for Nome in June of 1903, returning to the mining claim he had been working on. His father followed a month later. Arrangements were made for the rest of the family to move to Alaska on the last steamer of the season—all but George, who had a good job and was courting a young lady. But he, too, went to Nome three years later.

the beginning of their family, which increased every two years until the eleventh child was born in 1933. Most of the children were born in the reindeer camp tent—in the cold winter months, minus midwife or doctor.

In 1918 Seveck received word from Superintendent Shields of a Reindeer Fair to be held at Noatak village. For three weeks there were various forms of racing, for both the animals and the men; competition in many skills; lots of good food; and exchange of ideas about managing reindeer. Another Fair was held at Mary's Igloo near Cape Nome. Seveck and his sled deer made the three-week trip with Shields to this Fair over a long, rough trail. The year of these two Fairs was also the year that an epidemic swept the entire coast, taking the life of Shields and hundreds of others.

Seveck's leadership in the reindeer industry continued. Through the years he provided transportation and guide service to many travelers. Government surveyors called for his help in mapping new areas.

When, in 1928, the four big herds at Kivalina joined to become one, Seveck was chosen manager. He describes taking C. L. Andrews, the teacher at Kivalina, to Wainwright and Barrow in 1929. For the trip they had five sled deer and four sleds. All was well until a blizzard hit, then Andrews wanted to return for fear he would freeze to death. Fully confident of what he was doing, Seveck built a snow house whose comfort surprised Andrews. They cooked over the primus stove, had a good night's sleep, and wakened to a clear new day.

Off in the distance could be seen a herder, slowly and quietly walking along the outskirts of the herd, keeping notes on the arrival of each fawn. Andrews saw that Seveck had a special notice posted in the herder's tent:

Rules in Herding 1924

A man should be present when his turn comes for watching and herding sets on the time of the clock in the morning and in the evening.

No use the shepherd dog in fawning season.

Keep away the Eskimo dog from the herd. Do not leave the herd without some one watching them.

> *Chester Seveck*
> *Chief Herder*

Seveck retired from the reindeer industry in 1954 and was employed by Wein Airlines to promote tourism. He and his wife met and entertained visitors to Kotzebue during the summer, and traveled in the States during the winters. They were active in the Episcopal church, where Seveck had been a lay reader since 1917. His wife died in 1958. In 1959 Seveck married Helen. They traveled throughout the States to keep Alaska before the traveling public.

Whenever there was a celebration, Chester loved doing the Eskimo dances. His dancing, singing, and drumming were a delight to his people.

Chester Asakak Seveck died in January 1981 in Fairbanks, Alaska.

By 1906 the entire Lomen family had moved to Alaska—Carl, Alfred, Ralph, Harry, George, and Helen and both parents. The Lomen brothers prospered with a photographic studio and a drugstore, while the elder Lomen kept busy with legal work. All took part in local affairs.

First Major Sale to a Non-Native

In the summer of 1908, Walter C. Shields arrived in Nome as the Bureau of Education's new Reindeer Superintendent for the Northwest District of Alaska. He came directly from the Washington office. His coming ushered in

Superintendent Shields cooking over an alcohol stove during one of his inspection tours with Chester Seveck. Courtesy of National Archives.

a new era for the Eskimo and reindeer in northwestern Alaska.

Shields soon became a deerman, traveling everywhere with reindeer in the winter, and by boat in the summer. These trips extended from Barrow to the southern parts of Seward Peninsula. He was often accompanied by Carl Lomen, who was becoming increasingly interested in the reindeer business.

In the fall of 1913 Shields explained to Carl Lomen that Alfred Nilima, a Lapp, was completing his contract with the government and wanted to sell part of his herd so he could give more time to his mining properties. The government did not object to the sale of non-native herds to other non-natives.

Nilima was one of five Lapps whose reindeer ownership grew through several years of receiving their annual salaries from the federal government in the form of deer. The animals the Lapps received were both male and female, and the annual crop of fawns increased the herds rapidly. These herds were looked upon by the Lapps as investments to be used as they saw fit.

So it was that in September of 1914 Lomen and Company bought 1,200 reindeer from Nilima. That first major sale left many natives disillusioned and insecure. Already disheartened by Lapp herds, they believed that the sale of large numbers of reindeer to an outsider businessman would likely lead to big problems for their own herds. This sale of reindeer between non-native owners was to become the basis for contentions for the next 25 years.

There were 70,243 reindeer in Alaska in 1915 according to the Bureau of Education. Of these, 46,683 belonged to nearly 1,300 Eskimo owners, the government held 3,408, missions held 6,890, and Lapps and other non-natives owned 13,262. The largest number of non-native owned reindeer were in Lomen herds.

15

Reindeer Fairs

Problems associated with grazing area rights and the question of non-native ownership of herds continued. Practical men, like William Lopp and William Shields, continued their work on behalf of Eskimo reindeer herders.

Lopp had become Chief of the Alaska Bureau of Education. Shields organized the first Reindeer Fair in the fall of 1914. The local teachers, reindeer men, and superintendents were notified. He sent a list of questions to the various villages, encouraging participation of all in the Fair and competitions of herders and their reindeer.

The life of a herder was necessarily isolated, so the Reindeer Fairs provided welcome opportunities to meet old and new friends, and compare prized animals. They also gave the herders a chance to compare and to learn.

Of course the Fair had to be held in winter when there would be snow for traveling with the sleds and reindeer. Carl Lomen, in his book *Fifty Years in Alaska*, describes the Fair at Mary's Igloo.

The village of Igloo, 40 miles or so from Teller, made preparations months ahead for the second week in January 1915. Extra food was needed, and plenty of wood and stoves to prepare it for all the visitors. Tents were set up five miles from Igloo, on the Pilgrim River. Race trails were staked out.

Carl Lomen arrived with Shields and his party, including the Eskimo driver Tautook, who brought his special racer, Dynamite. Starting from Nome, they spent three nights

Thomas Siquenuk and his reindeer at the 1916 Reindeer Fair. Courtesy of Glenbow Archives, Calgary, Alberta.

Walter C. Shields

Walter C. Shields came to be Superintendent of the Northwest District of the Bureau of Education in 1910. He became well-traveled and highly respected throughout his district, capable with both dog-team and reindeer. Native Alaskans placed a lot of confidence in his supervision.

One example of his efforts was the establishment of Reindeer Fairs. Reproduced here is the text of the letter Shields sent to all the villages.

Schoolroom

Who will you send to the Fair to represent your herds?

Will you have the largest sled deer? The best looking? The tamest new sled deer, broken since September first?

Will you have the best made hardwood racing sled? Best hardwood flat sled? Best soft wood sled?

Can your men make the best collar? The best halter? Who can make a new kind of halter better than the old one? Have you the best Lapp style harness? Best single tree harness? Who can make a new kind of harness that is better than the old kind? Who can make harness of deer leather?

Is there a good reindeer dog at your herd? If so bring him along and we will see if he is the best in Alaska.

Can the women of your village, or the school girls make good deer skin clothing? Tanned well and sewed well, with sinew. Bring your parkies, mittens, mukluks, pants and sleeping bags, all of reindeer skin.

Can some delegate's wife, or the schoolgirls make a banner for your men to carry to the Fair so that everybody on the trail may know where they have come from?

Are any of your herders very good shots with the rifle? Can they win a prize shooting at 50 yards? At 100 yards? At 200 yards?

Have you a good man with the lasso? He may be a good man at his home herd but can he lasso with the other men from all the other herds?

How fast can your men load and lash a sled with a travelling outfit so that snow can't get in and the load cannot get loose? How quickly can your men harness a good deer, hitch him to the sled, and start off? We will see how many seconds it takes to do these things.

Eskimos and their deer at the 1916 Reindeer Fair. Courtesy of Glenbow Archives, Calgary, Alberta.

Walter C. Shields (*continued*)

How many pounds of dead weight can your strongest deer pull for 200 yards, without any help from the driver? How much can two deer hitched to one sled pull? If you have the strongest sled deer in Alaska bring him to the Fair. We want to see him pull.

How many deer and sleds can a good man handle alone? Have you a man who can handle about five behind sleds, without having lots of trouble?

How many of these races will your men win: Five miles, one deer, 150 pounds load besides the man, 200 pounds load for two deer, 400 pounds for four deer. Five mile race, two behind sleds. Five mile race for eight deer hitched to one sled driven by two men. One man with two behind sleds over a very bad trail, through brush and deep snow. Will your men win the 10 mile races with one and two deer? Have you a new sled deer broken since September first that can run in a race?

Have you a good man to run on snowshoes? We will have a snowshoe race. There will be another race for men on snowshoes, each man to lead a deer by the halter. Some men always have to drag deer by the neck. We will see what your boys can do.

How many of your men have stayed their full time at the herd the past year? How many of the herders' wives have stayed at the herd with their husbands? Who has kept the best papers?

Have you some men who know a lot about the reindeer business? Send them to the Fair. We want to hear them talk about it. Send a man who can get up before us all and tell us true things that he knows himself about the reindeer. We want to learn everything that your men know about the deer and we want to tell them everything that we know, so that he may come back to you and tell you many new things.

Now what are you going to do about the Fair? Will you send some good men, and some good sleds, and some good harness so that you may be proud of your herd and your reindeer men?

Walter Shields

Shields' death during the influenza epidemic in the winter of 1918-1919 was a blow to the whole reindeer industry. His organizational ability was irreplaceable.

Deer pulling heavy load during the 1916 Fair. Courtesy of Glenbow Archives, Calgary, Alberta.

on the way to Igloo, the temperature hovering around thirty degrees below zero.

The next to arrive at Igloo were from Deering, 136 miles away, and the next were from Shishmaref, still farther away. Then came Dagny Brevig, daughter of the missionary at Teller. Just eighteen years old, she had grown up at the mission and spoke Eskimo fluently. She was a valuable and popular interpreter. Now she arrived by dog team, driven by Anikartuk. Pastor Brevig arrived the next day with the delegation from Teller. That evening more than a hundred people gathered in the Igloo schoolhouse.

That first evening in camp the men walked a mile to the hot sulphur springs, so hot that they had to stir the water with a paddle before getting in. A frame building covered the pool. After swimming they sat and sweated it out in the steam room, then went outside for a roll in the snow.

The first item of interest on the Fair program was a butchering demonstration: three different methods by Eskimo deermen, then another by a member of the U.S. Department of Agriculture who happened to be visiting.

There was a rifle-shooting contest at 50 yards, then 100 yards; then a burden race, with 250 pounds of sand for five miles. There was lassoing of deer; racing with one, two, or four deer. Many different handcrafts were represented in displays of sleds, harness, and clothing.

In one test of skill, the contestant, at a signal, had to enter the herd and rope, throw, harness, hitch up, and drive a hornless, unbroken bull one-half mile up the river and return to the starting point, then unhitch and remove the harness without help. Lomen described the contest to drive a wild deer.

This contest was the acid test of a man's ability as a reindeer man. When a wild bull was lassoed, it fought to escape and the driver was forced to throw it. When the assistant brought up a sled, the maneuvering to harness the struggling animal was laughable and very exciting. No sooner was the harness fastened than the bull started to run and would throw the driver all about. One of the smallest contestants lassoed the largest bull in the herd and found it impossible to drive the beast at all. He threw the bull alongside the sled, which he tipped on edge, and then rolled Mr. Bull right onto the sled, tied him down, so he could not roll off, and started up the river, pulling the sled himself. I laughed until the tears rolled down my cheeks. And the usually phlegmatic Eskimo were in stitches, too. [12]

Each owner saved his fastest and best deer for the concluding event: the eleven-mile one-deer race. The winning time was 45 minutes, 38 seconds, with the best four coming in only three-and-a-half seconds apart.

Reindeer Fair participants leading reindeer during snowshoe race. Courtesy of Glenbow Archives, Calgary, Alberta.

A 10-mile sled race during the 1917 Reindeer Fair. Courtesy of Glenbow Archives, Calgary, Alberta.

The 1914 Reindeer Fair was a great success and plans were made immediately for another Fair the following year. Again it was an exciting time of competition and learning. A third Fair was held in 1917, with added events and new displays of carved walrus ivory and brightly decorated sleds and harness, as well as clothing worn by the herders. Old time fire-making contests were held. And men competed in a snow-melting contest, by using only one match, whittling kindling, lighting it, and melting a tin cupful of snow. The ability to melt snow was important. On the trail, men could chill their stomachs if they ate the unmelted snow.

In 1918, Chester Seveck was notified by Shields of the Fair to be held at Noatak village. What a gathering that must have been! In his book, *Longest Reindeer Herder*, Seveck lists the villages that were invited to send herders: Barrow, Wainwright, Icy Cape, Point Hope, Kivalina, Kobuk, Selawik, Buckland, Kotzebue, Deering, Candle, Noorvik, Shishmaref. And of course herders at Noatak took part. This Fair lasted three weeks.

Afterward, Seveck took Shields to another reindeer Fair at Mary's Igloo. It took three weeks to make the trip, with very tough traveling. The races and competitions created much the same excitement as at Noatak.

Seveck had left his wife with her parents in Kotzebue, so after the Fair at Igloo he drove his sled deer to get her and return to his herd at Deering. They arrived in late April.

In that same year, the young men of Alaska were inducted into the U.S. Army. On their trip to Fort Lewis, near Tacoma, Washington, an epidemic of flu broke out. Thirty-five of the ship's passengers and crew died. The ship left the epidemic in its wake at Nome.

Many whites and more than 700 Eskimos died as the disease spread up and down the coast. Scores of the ablest Eskimo reindeer men died. The death of Walter Shields was a tremendous loss to the reindeer industry. He had earned the respect of everyone, and his leadership had smoothed over many clashes.

16

Controversy

In its report for 1917-1918, the Bureau of Education indicated that Lomen and Company's efforts could benefit the reindeer industry. The company was developing a market for reindeer outside Alaska and buying steers from native owners with large herds, thereby increasing the local market for smaller herds.

In the same report, John F. A. Strong, the Governor of the Territory of Alaska, stated that he believed reindeer meat could increase the food supply of the United States as a whole. He thought the reindeer industry should be encouraged among whites, so long as native endeavors did not suffer.

Management of Eskimo Reindeer

In 1917, William T. Lopp, still Chief of the Alaska Division of the Bureau of Education, recommended that Nunivak Island be set apart as a reindeer reserve for the natives.

Eskimo hauling reindeer meat to Nome market. Courtesy of Glenbow Archives, Calgary, Alberta.

Clarence L. Andrews

Out of his own experience, Clarence Leroy Andrews could understand, more than many city dwellers, a harder, simpler life spent closer to nature. He spent his younger years, from 1864 to 1882, in the Willamette Valley of Oregon, a state only since 1859, in the livestock business and farming. And from 1883 to 1889 he lived on the little populated stock ranges of eastern Oregon, where extremes of weather could greatly affect your livelihood.

The year 1892 found Andrews in Alaska, where he immediately became interested in the reindeer project. He was a customs agent in Alaska from 1897 to 1899. Later, in 1917, Andrews traveled the coast from St. Michael to Point Barrow with Walter Shields, who was then Superintendent of the School and Reindeer Service.

On that trip Andrews and Shields also visited the Chukchi reindeer people of Siberia at three places. This journey added to Andrews's understanding of the demands of life in the far north. His understanding grew still more during the nearly seven years he spent, from 1923 until 1929, in the School and Reindeer Service.

Andrews wrote a number of books and articles about the Eskimos, the reindeer industry, and life in the Arctic. In *The Eskimo and His Reindeer in Alaska*, Andrews revealed his views on education:

The Eskimo of one hundred years ago had an education of his own. It was sufficient for him to live in the land in which his lot was cast. He knew far better how to do it than any white man in the world, even though civilization furnishes better weapons and equipment. . . . The white race, with their education, came, destroyed the Eskimo's means of living, and with it went his education to a great extent. Now the white race is confronted with the necessity of giving the Eskimo an education that will enable him to live under his new conditions. Education means the ability to live.

An ardent supporter of the Native reindeer industry, Andrews wrote about the Eskimos and their reindeer as late as 1948. He died in 1952.

The Department of Interior rejected the recommendation. In 1920 the Lomens established a trading post and small herd of reindeer on Nunivak.

Between 1918 and 1920, Lopp urged a new herd management system. Instead of individual owners herding their own deer, a village selected herders to manage combined herds. These reindeer associations, or cooperatively managed herds, helped solve some management and grazing area problems, at least for the time being.

Clarence L. Andrews, a teacher and reindeer supervisor from 1923 to 1929, recorded one of his trips to check the herd at Wainwright. At this roundup there were about 100 owners, each with an individual mark. The difficulty of keeping the records and apportioning the increase indicated the need for forming a company of herd owners. So, after the reindeer count was completed, articles of agreement were drawn up. The Eskimo herders met together and agreed that the fawns should be distributed, after counting, based on the number of shares (one for each deer) that the owner already had in the company. All the deer in the herd would have one mark.

To carry out company business, a president and board of directors were elected. The following evening, the seven men elected to office met again to make plans for the coming year. They appointed chief herders, assistant herders, and a manager; decided on herders' pay and camp allowances; and attended to other details.

Wainwright village also started a native store. The success of this store attracted a

Mackenzie River Drive

An interesting transaction occurred in 1926 between Carl Lomen and the Canadian government. Lomen sold 3,000 reindeer for $195,000, including delivery to the Mackenzie River area in Canada's Northwest Territory. That meant driving the herd over 1600 miles of unmapped country across the top of the continent.

Lomen contacted Andy Bahr, retired and living in Seattle, to take charge of this drive. Bahr was one of the herders who had come over from Lapland in 1898 when the Yukon miners were thought to be threatened with starvation. Now 63 years old, he accepted the challenge.

On December 26, 1929, the village of Nabactoolik on Kotzebue Sound was the starting point. The herd of 3,000 reindeer, with Eskimos driving dog teams with loaded sleds, and Laplanders with reindeer-drawn sleds, started on the long trek.

The Great Trek, by Max Miller, is a colorful account of the struggle to move this herd of 3,000 animals through violent winter storms and heat of summers with torturing insects, with hungry predators always on the perimeter. It was a "living hell" for both animals and men. Their only contact was by an occasional airplane. They reached the Mackenzie River on March 6, 1937—after five years and two months on the way.

The final count was 2,375, of which only ten percent wore ear tags, indicating they were in the original herd. The rest were born during the drive. When fawning time came in spring, the count increased and the original contract was filled.

---

trader who opened a rival trading post. The trader's financial backer, a wealthy ship owner and trader, bragged about "what I am doing for the natives." But he also took advantage of the Eskimos' lack of business knowledge. By not providing an invoice for one lot of goods he left the Eskimos to guess at fair prices for individual items.

While the village population could support the two stores, the backer's way of doing business nearly ruined the Eskimo store. Here is what Andrews had to say about the backer:

His sharp practice in methods of doing business brought disaster to the native establishment which was not repaired for many years. Such practices were not uncommon in that country.[13]

A study of reindeer herding in northwestern Alaska, published in 1980, expressed the view that the stock-ownership system had other problems in addition to unscrupulous business practices of whites.[14] The small size of the local market combined with payment for services with meat meant little cash was generated from reindeer meat sales to pay company expenses. Also, the original shares were based on the total number of animals contributed to the nucleus herd, rather than on the number of breeding females—the animals that made possible the herd increase.

The records kept did not distinguish among bulls, breeding females, and fawns. Shares were added to an Eskimo's account for labor and other services to the company as well as for a portion of the annual percentage increase in the herd. In this way, shares for individual owners grew more rapidly than did the number of reindeer: herds increased faster on the books than they did in real life.

Lomen Marketing Efforts

While the government tried to work out the best management system for native-owned reindeer, Lomen and Company prepared for extensive exportation of reindeer products. In the summer of 1920, they explored the natural "freezers" that could be built into the frozen tundra. The storage shaft built by an Eskimo in the Buckland area was 3 by 4 by 20 feet deep. Outdoor temperature was 72 degrees Fahrenheit the day it was checked. Three feet down it was 30 degrees, and on the bottom it was 23 degrees.

The following winter the Lomens had a small room excavated. Meat they stored in the room kept well until the summer.

Elephant Point, on Eschscholtz Bay, was then developed. Six new storage rooms were constructed, each 18 by 36 by 7 feet high. Total storage capacity: 10,000 reindeer carcasses. The first winter 2,000 animals were butchered and stored to test the facility. The second year 8,000 carcasses were stored for summer shipment.

The facility at Elephant Point provided easy access for shipping, and was centrally located for driving the herds for butchering. A narrow-gauge railway carried meat from the far end of the storage tunnel to the scows, or lighters, used to carry the cargos from the beach to the ships that would take them to the States.

Elephant Point was a complete complex of corrals, a large abattoir (slaughterhouse), holding and boning rooms, bins for salting and stacking hides, and living quarters for a large crew. Other locations were similar, but none as large as Elephant Point. Shipments increased, except in 1919: 10,650 pounds were shipped in 1916; 33,000 pounds in 1917; 99,000 pounds in 1918; 37,000 pounds in 1919; and 257,000 pounds in 1920. By 1920 there were distributors in Seattle, Portland, the twin cities (probably a reference to Minneapolis and St. Paul), Oklahoma City, Chicago, New York, and Boston.

The Lomens purchased and outfitted their own fleet of ships: the *Sierra*, the *Donaldson*, the *Baldwin*, and the *Silver Wave*. They owned tugs for lightering service: the *Genevieve*, the *Dayton*, the *Wave*, and the *Sawtooth*. They handled freight for the Alaska Steamship Company in addition to their own freight.

Lomen's first reindeer to be processed for meat to market in the States, Nome, Alaska, August 4, 1915. Courtesy of Glenbow Archives, Calgary, Alberta.

The Lomens' Elephant Point facility prepared reindeer meat and other products for market. It included the Lomens' largest underground freezer storage and housing for workers. Courtesy of University of Alaska Archives, Palmer Collection.

Continuing Problems

Native reindeer herds supplied local markets. The consumption of reindeer meat dropped in Alaska as miners and the merchants that served them moved away from the mining areas in the 1910s. This was a real blow to Eskimo reindeer owners. Their herds increased faster than before, and they needed more grazing areas. So did the Lomens.

Effort was made to relieve the oversupply of native-owned reindeer in 1920. The U.S.S. *Boxer*, which brought school supplies north to Alaska, was charged with taking reindeer carcasses back south on behalf of the natives. Thus, for a number of years the native herders were able to market animals beyond their local areas. This probably helped to slow up conflict between Eskimos and the Lomens over range land.

By 1922 there were approximately 259,000 reindeer in Alaska. Two-thirds were in native hands. The Bureau of Education introduced a joint stock ownership system for the natives, in an attempt to solve problems that the large number of reindeer only made more difficult to resolve.

Problems included questions about inheritance and sales of deer, how to deal with the rapid increase in reindeer identifying marks, and disputes over range use and herd handling. Under the joint stock ownership system, or cooperative ownership system, all the animals owned by the people of one village were herded together by paid herders. The chief herder was chosen by the community and given responsibility for supervision of all day-to-day activities.

Another effort was made to establish an outlet for reindeer products via the newly completed Alaska Railroad. Ben B. Mozee was the Reindeer Service employee who led a drive of 1,437 reindeer in 1922 to the interior railroad area of Cantwell, not far from Mt. McKinley. Unfortunately, by 1928 the Cantwell reindeer industry had failed, due to predators, lack of constant herding, personnel changes, and losses to caribou herds. (The final remnants of this Cantwell herd became residents at the University of Alaska's Agricultural Experimental Farm at Fairbanks.)

The system of joint stock ownership continued for about 25 years, but gradually declined. It seems that the owners decided the summer roundups were unnecessary—and too expensive—and that the winter roundup was sufficient. As the herds continued to increase, they figured this would happen without close herding. The peak years were the early 1930s. But, as the Depression deepened, there was virtually no wage labor available and many herds were abandoned. By then the government and the owners realized that stock ownership companies were not managing the herds effectively. The government initiated a change back to the original ownership by individuals.

17

Conflicting Interests

Before his death in 1918, Walter C. Shields had expressed the belief that few marketing problems would arise so long as white owners of reindeer continued their current policies. But he had thought that problems were likely to arise over grazing issues as the herds of native and non-native owners continued to increase—and overlap.

Grazing Rights and Ownership

It turned out that Shields was certainly right about grazing issues. The thriving reindeer became the center of a growing controversy over grazing land desired by both natives and non-natives.

The Lomen family took over the best shipping points on the Seward Peninsula one by one. First it was Kotzebue Sound, with the purchase of Nilima's herd in 1914. Then it was Golovin Bay when they purchased 1,000 head from the Swedish Mission there. Next it was Port Clarence when they purchased 319 deer from the mission at Teller.

While all of these were vital points for shipping, of more immediate importance to Eskimos was the fact that Lomen herds were introduced into what had been the principal grazing areas for the hard-earned Eskimo

Reindeer herd at Lomen corral across from Teller. Courtesy of Glenbow Archives, Calgary, Alberta.

herds. And the Lomens continued to buy reindeer.

In the five years after they purchased from the mission at Teller they bought 6,174 more deer from immigrant herders. They also, in Lomen's words, "succeeded to other herds at Kotzebue, Teller, Golovin, Egavik, and Buckland."[15] These numbers do not include the ample yearly increases.

The increase in both Eskimo and Lomen herds put pressure on the available range land. Those reindeer superintendents who sympathized with the Lomens' reindeer efforts agreed that grazing areas could be shared by native and non-native herds. This suited the Lomens, but at every roundup time native owners found their animals absorbed and marked into Lomen herds that pushed onto prior native-only areas.

The Lomens maintained that a fair division of the increase in mixed herds was worked out: the new fawns were distributed according to the number of female deer belonging to the various owners. In theory this was a good system. Eskimo owners would receive fawns in proportion to the number of females they contributed to breeding. But as Lomen herds continued to increase and cross over into areas formerly used by individual Eskimo herds, many Eskimo herds became disorganized and their owners were at a loss as to how to cope with the white man's way of doing business.

The Lomens believed that their presence in Alaska benefited rather than deprived the Eskimos. Eskimos—as well as those whites who favored a native-only reindeer industry—took a dim view of the Lomen activities. The problem of grazing rights was magnified, as Shields foresaw could happen.

Further Lomen Marketing Efforts

Developing the market for reindeer meat was not easy for the Lomens. The first shipment to New York was confiscated and destroyed by the State Conservation Commission. They held that the reindeer was a game animal, making its sale illegal.

There were colorful promotion schemes to bring reindeer meat to the attention of the public in the States. Lomen replied to columnist Heywood Broun who had written of his surprise at being served reindeer meat in the dining car of a train. In his letter, Lomen wrote that Santa Claus had been hit by the high cost of living. Since Santa's herds in Alaska had increased to more than 325,000 animals he had decided to place some of his choicest animals on the market. He had selected the speediest animals for his sled and was marketing the surplus, thus paying for gifts for his sack and at the same time supplying the people of the United States with an additional food product. This exchange in 1924 increased sales immediately.

Contracts also were made to supply live reindeer together with Santa and his Eskimo helpers to several shopping centers prior to the holiday season. Reindeer were prepared for subscribers in Brooklyn, Boston, Philadelphia, Detroit, St. Louis, Kansas City, Los Angeles, San Francisco, and Portland, Oregon. Preparation of the reindeer meant, primarily, to teach them to eat wheat, rolled oats, and alfalfa tips instead of their natural foods. Young animals, with well-shaped antlers, were handled daily until they became very tame.

Anticipation was built up by daily newspapers, with imaginary letters from children to the editors. At last, the first shipment of live reindeer reached Seattle in October of 1926. There were 76 deer with 16 Eskimo and Lapp drivers. All left the ship in utmost secrecy—on their way to various destinations.

Those going to Portland, San Francisco, and Los Angeles were trucked to a farm near Portland to become acclimated. *The Oregon Journal* covered the arrival of Santa, his reindeer, and drivers. When the reindeer team

Reindeer fawns. Courtesy of Glenbow Archives, Calgary, Alberta.

pulled Santa and his sled (mounted on hidden wheels) down the streets of Portland, crowds were almost beyond control. A great success!

When Lomen and Company organized in 1914 they had the backing of Jafet Lindeberg, a Norwegian miner who had grown wealthy during the early days of the Nome Gold Rush. His support ended in 1921 when his banking investments failed. Lomen Reindeer and Trading Corporation was then formed, the first of several reorganizations by the family and their supporters. Carl Lomen opened sales offices in New York and Seattle for promotion purposes, but was never able to secure enough capital to handle all the problems that arose.

Nonetheless, from 1928 to 1930 the Lomens shipped to the United States 30,000 carcasses of meat and thousands of reindeer hides for the manufacture of gloves. In 1929 the Great Depression hit and meat prices tumbled. Cattle and sheep men, shipping carloads of animals to market, received less money in full payment of their shipments than was needed for the freight bills.

Eskimo Accomplishments Praised

Through the 1910s and 1920s the Eskimo reindeer owners had many supporters of their cause. One of them—Clarence L. Andrews—wrote numerous letters and articles that testify to the abuse of natives. From his writings it is evident he believed that Eskimos had a culture suited to their life and that domestic reindeer were a useful addition to their resources after outsiders came along and disrupted the environment. In one of his books, Andrews wrote:

The Eskimos have been severely censured by their critics, the corporations, and other non-native owners, charging that they do not have good appliances and do not care for their herds. Considering that they did not have other than what they had earned by their wages in reindeer or other manner, while the corporations boast of millions of dollars invested, the native has done remarkably well, and until the heresy of 'open herding' was introduced, and his deer were mixed with the white men's herds, to his loss and damage, he has accomplished much for a man only one lifetime removed from a hunter on the sea. [16]

18

Resolution

Eskimo interests and white—mainly Lomen —interests in reindeer and grazing rights were on a collision course. Eskimo reindeer management became more difficult as the Lomens acted to make a major commercial success of their reindeer operation.

The Department of the Interior approved an order late in 1928 setting aside Kotzebue Peninsula for the Lomen Reindeer Corporation to conduct experiments to eradicate the warble fly. The Alaska Reindeer Service had not been consulted. Then early in 1929 the Lomen corporation applied for a grazing lease to include all of Kotzebue Peninsula. The protest was so strong that the Lomens withdrew their application.

Changing of the Guard

The Secretary of the Interior signed an order in 1929 that placed responsibility for reindeer matters in the hands of Alaska's Governor George Parks. This ended the Bureau of Education involvement with reindeer.

Within six months after administration became the responsibility of his office, the governor sent his recommendations to E. K. Burlew, who was an administrative assistant to the Secretary of the Interior. Parks was convinced that the federal government should reorganize administration of the reindeer industry and continue direct work only until natives could manage on their own. After that he believed the government should continue in an advisory role only. (This is basically the situation today. The federal role is primarily advisory, although the Bureau of Land Management is responsible for range protection and grazing permit assignments.)

While Parks was working out his plans, protests against the Lomen activities flooded into Washington. Disputes over ownership and grazing rights poured into the Department of the Interior all through the 1930s. The Reindeer Service protested; the native reindeer associations and the various church and missionary groups pressured the Secretary of the Interior to take action. The federal government sent an investigating team to Alaska almost every year over this 10-year period.

The Lomens proposed in 1931 an organization plan for reindeer on the Seward Peninsula. This organization would give their corporation a percentage ownership and a voice in handling all of the deer in the whole area, including St. Lawrence Island. The Lomens would receive part of the government appropriations that for forty years had been made for the native peoples. Objections were raised. The Lomens would have the advantage over other traders who dealt with the natives. The government policy of helping natives to manage their own affairs would be destroyed. Carl Lomen defended the plan as a better way of managing the large numbers of native-owned reindeer and extending the market for reindeer products.

Reindeer Council Ineffective

Lomen's plan was rejected by a newly formed council that was intended to resolve conflicts locally. The Reindeer Council resulted from hearings in Washington, D.C., in 1931. The hearings committee also recommended roundups to establish ownership and the number of reindeer, transfer of reindeer to separate native and non-native ranges, more equitable marketing methods, and expansion of the Alaska Reindeer Service.

The Reindeer Council included the Governor of Alaska as ex-officio chairman, the Chief of the Alaska Division of the Office of Indian Affairs, the General Supervisor of the Alaska Reindeer Service, a representative chosen by and from the Eskimo owners, and a representative of the Lomen interests.[17]

The Superintendent of the Northwestern School District was to supervise the selection of the representative for the Eskimo owners. However, the superintendent did not receive word from Juneau until after breakup—the time of spring when frozen rivers thaw into ice jams and land trails become mud and slush. This made it impossible for him to communicate with the owners before the date of the council meeting.

At the first convening of the council there were 10 sessions. One native member, from the Teller area, arrived in time for the sixth session.

The Eskimos, who owned 70 percent of all reindeer in Alaska, had only one vote (or one-half vote each if they sent two representatives). The Lomens were given representation on this five-vote council while other whites (including Lapps) who owned more deer than they did had no representation.

Benjamin B. Mozee, an ardent supporter of the Eskimos, who held the appointive position of General Supervisor of the Alaska Reindeer Service from 1928 to 1933, saw this as a real discrimination in favor of the Lomens, and such an unrepresentative body as a negative influence on the reindeer industry.[18]

According to Mozee, in 1929 Judge Lomen said to him that any government agent who opposed the Lomens had been dismissed or forced out of the Reindeer Service. And a member of a government investigation team asserted that any man who would not cooperate with the Lomens could be removed.

Matters continued to get worse. In 1932, Andrews wrote that the reindeer industry on the Seward Peninsula was in chaos. The Lomens tried to force native owners into a partnership in order to make the natives liable for debts owed by the Lomen corporation. When the Eskimos protested, the Lomen corporation advised the administrative assistant to the Secretary of the Interior against allowing natives to interfere with movements that influenced their deer.

The Lomens continued to sell deer carcasses without properly accounting for whose deer were slaughtered. They charged the native herd owners a grazing fee for use of the range that had formerly belonged to the natives.

Mozee constantly ran afoul of the strategies of the Lomen enterprises. They succeeded in having him removed.

Eskimo Leaders Speak Out

The *Alaska Press*, Juneau, Alaska, dated September 21, 1934, carried a lengthy petition to the U.S. government, signed by William Allokeuk, Allokeuk and Konuk Herd; John Sinnock, Shishmaref Herd; Louis Tungwenuk, Cape Reindeer Company; and Robert

Etuktituk, Teller Mission Reindeer Company. In great detail these Eskimo herd owners described the many years of abuse by the Lomens and their supporters. They named government agents who had been influenced by the powerful Lomen family to protect Lomen interests. They described the position of Judge Lomen:

For the past ten years the District Court and the Grand Juries were practically under the domination of Judge G. J. Lomen, principal organizer of the Lomen Company and long time head and legal advisor. Judge Lomen appointed all the United States Commissioners in the District during that period—most of them are still in office. [19]

The maneuverings of Judge Lomen explained why there had never been an investigation of the disputes between the Eskimos and the Lomen interests. When the Lomens needed the signature of an Eskimo on a legal document, they secured it by insisting it was for the good of all, with threat of jail or other punishment if he did not sign it. Eskimos could not read or understand the legal language and were put in the position of having to trust the interpretation of Lomen and his cohorts.

The signers of the petition asked for an investigation of the alleged abuse of an Eskimo of Nunivak Island. This person reportedly was kidnapped by Carl Lomen and John Hegness, tied in the hold of a Lomen schooner, and seldom fed or given water enroute to home. Echoes of this atrocity are heard every once in a while to this day. It would be interesting to find a record of the details, which seem to have been buried with other damaging evidence.

The storm of protests that reached Washington brought more investigations. Shakeups and internal reorganization in Washington reflected these investigations.

The director of the Division of Education sent a confidential report to the Secretary of

Typical grazing scene. Government herd at Sinruk, 1910. Courtesy of Glenbow Archives, Calgary, Alberta.

the Interior in June 1933. He asked whether the government was engaged in the reindeer enterprise for the economic and social development of the Alaskan native, or for the benefit of private commercial interests.

The Secretary of the Interior sent Roy Nash, a special agent, to investigate. Nash's confidential report seven months later vindicated the people who had for so long protested Lomen activities. Among the several recommendations by Nash was the immediate and complete separation of native-owned and white-owned herds. He wanted the Lomen corporation stopped in its tracks.

The Lomens recognized, by 1934, that they no longer had any large-scale market in the United States, and that the local Alaskan markets would be well supplied by native herds. It was time to recover as much as they could of their holdings. They listed their holdings of reindeer herds as valued at about $4,325,000 and other reindeer enterprises at about $4,600,000. But the Baldwins, financial backers of the Lomens, offered to sell all to the U.S. government for $950,000.

Reindeer Act Restores Native Herds

Final hearings were held in the spring and summer of 1936. Legislation was urged for controlled grazing leases by the Reindeer Service, for restricted property status for native-owned reindeer, and for elimination of white-owned herds from needed ranges by fair and equitable means. An investigator was assigned to assess the social and economic status of natives of northwestern Alaska. The investigator found them so heavily in debt to the trading posts that they were no longer free agents.

That same year Congress appointed a Reindeer Appraisal Committee (also known as the Rachford Committee). They worked closely with members of the Alaska Reindeer Service. By August 1939, Congress appropriated funds that were authorized under the Reindeer Act. Instead of the $2,000,000 authorized, the appropriation was only $720,000 for the purchase of non-native-owned reindeer and facilities, and $75,000 for administrative expenses.

Final roundups were necessary for settlement, superceding estimates made by the survey teams. These were completed during the winter of 1939-1940. Charles G. Burdick was appointed Special Representative of the Secretary of Interior on November 1, 1939, and he was given the responsibility for carrying out provisions of the Reindeer Act.

This chronology and accounting concludes one era in the reindeer industry in Alaska. It ushered in a new era of reconstruction—of learning together about the compatibility of environment and the domestic reindeer industry. The fifty years following 1939 will make an interesting history for another chronicler.

Epilogue

When Sheldon Jackson introduced domestic reindeer to Alaskan Eskimos, he visualized a supply of food and clothing that would be close at hand for each village, with the possibility of commercial trade in due time. But his first concern was sustaining life through the long, dark, and bitter-cold winters of that area and of that time. Few white men survived the winters of those years without the help of Eskimos.

The reindeer industry took on a new focus when the federal government passed the Reindeer Act of 1937. With the final roundup and count of the reindeer in the winter of 1939-40, domestic reindeer in Alaska were returned to Native ownership, as originally intended. The story of the Eskimos and their reindeer in the years after 1940 is complex; a story I did not set out to tell here.

Still, there are questions the reader may have that can be answered briefly. On January 8, 1988, I spoke by telephone with Dr. Bob Dieterich on the Seward Peninsula, where he was working among the reindeer herds. With some twenty years of reindeer experience with the Institute of Arctic Biology of the University of Alaska, he was able to summarize the current situation.

How many reindeer are there now in Alaska? About 30,000 in some 18 privately owned herds, mostly on the Seward Peninsula and Unalaska.

Is there an association of reindeer herders? Yes. Larry Davis is president of the Native Reindeer Herders' Association. Jake Olanna is the executive director. Jake Olanna is an appointee of the Department of Interior and salaried by the Bureau of Indian Affairs. Both officers are Eskimos.

Is there still a government model herd? No. Some of the herds are investments of the village corporations. The Native villages were organized throughout the state into thirteen regional corporations after settlement of Native land claims in the Alaska Native Claims Settlement Act (ANCSA), 1971. The thirteenth corporation is composed of Eskimos, Aleuts, Athabascans, Tlingits, and Haida with at least one-quarter Native blood who live outside the state of Alaska.

To start a new herd, a person "leases" the number of animals wanted from an established herd. When the increase of the "leased" herd numbers enough animals to sustain itself, the original number of animals is returned to the originating herd. The new herd could be from 300 to 500 animals, but the best size to start with is 500 for individual family use. There is a growing interest in owning small herds for commercial purposes, which would start with 1,000 animals to be commercially profitable.

Herding is done primarily with snow machines and three-wheelers; helicopters are used occasionally. However, some owners are going back to herding on foot, referred to as "close herding," as originally initiated by Jackson and the Lapps. There is also some use of horses and dogs. (Appendix A, beginning on page 90, describes herding as well as characteristics of domestic reindeer.)

Migration of the Western Arctic caribou in the northeastern portion of the Seward Peninsula is closing in on the grazing areas of the domestic herds in the northwestern portion of the Peninsula. This movement of the wild deer will invariably be a magnet; the domestic animals will respond to the "call of the wild" that decreases the domestic herds measurably. With the help of government game management, the herders try to predict movement of the caribou and keep the domestic animals in other areas.

Modern advances have brought so many comforts that life in the far north is a very different story than when Jackson first arrived. But the nine months of winter are still long and dark. And cold is really COLD! Lots of good protein—and cash to secure other needs—can be harvested from a crop of well-tended reindeer. The raising of reindeer is totally compatible with the environment and is local. And the reindeer are a renewable resource.

Are Alaskan Native families showing interest in the reindeer industry? Yes. Learning more about reindeer husbandry, disease control, and supervision of grazing areas and working with the agencies of land and wild life management, a new generation of reindeer owners and herders is slowly but surely establishing itself.

Appendices

Characteristics of Domestic Reindeer

The description here is based on an article in the University of Alaska's School of Agricultural Resources and Land Management periodical, Agroborealis, *January 1980, and an article in the quarterly* Alaska Geographic, *Summer, 1981.*

First, it is well to distinguish between the domestic reindeer and caribou that live in the Arctic. Both the domestic reindeer and caribou that live in the far north belong to the deer family *Cervidae* and the genus *Rangifer*. The two are distinguishable in a number of ways, and some scientists identify two species: *Rangifer tarandus*, the domestic reindeer, and *Rangifer arcticus*, wild reindeer. The wild reindeer are the northern, Barren Ground caribou of the tundra and taiga forest areas.

Domestic reindeer are considerably smaller than caribou. The reindeer weigh from 175 to 300 pounds, and stand about three feet tall at the shoulder. Caribou weigh up to about 660 pounds and stand as much as four feet tall. Both male and female reindeer and caribou have antlers, the only members of the deer family for which this is true.

The coat of the reindeer is thick, with hard, brittle outer hairs covering a dense underfur. The hide has been used for centuries in far northern countries to make clothing effective against the cold.

Large lateral hooves allow the feet to spread on snow or on soft ground. Moving through packed snow, they make a crackling sound apparently caused by the popping of the tendons in their five-toed hooves. When they are frightened a gland between their toes leaves a warning scent that is instantly recognized by others of the herd.

A primary difference in reindeer and caribou behavior is that reindeer can be kept in captivity, while caribou cannot. Introduced at the end of the nineteenth century, reindeer are newcomers to Alaska, coming from many generations of captivity in Siberia. Their wild cousins, the caribou, have existed in Alaska, and other areas of the Arctic, for thousands of years.

The migrations of caribou from the spring range where calving occurs to summer range, to winter range, and back to spring range can interfere with maintenance of domestic reindeer herds. Reindeer do not discriminate between their own herd and caribou herds, and if given a chance will join caribou when a herd is nearby, and will be absorbed into the wild with cross-breeding. Reindeer also will mingle with other reindeer herds. Careful management of domestic reindeer is necessary to avoid such losses by keeping individual reindeer herds separated. The early reindeer herds in Alaska were held in controlled areas, and moved to new forage areas by the herders and their dogs.

During the long winter, reindeer moss

(*Cladonia rangiferina*) furnishes the rich nutrients needed. The deer can detect its presence under snow up to three feet deep, and can paw for it with their sharp cloven hooves.

The winter storms that leave frozen crusts can prove disastrous when the ice is too thick to break through. At such time there is heavy loss from starvation.

The fresh greens of early spring are eagerly sought by the herds. Special favorites are the Alaska cotton and the tundra willow, which grows only five or six inches tall.

The grazing herd thrives on tender foliage and grass of summer, and as winter approaches it is time to seek out the mosses and lichens again.

The modern use of snow-machines, airplanes, and helicopters is being reviewed and questioned. The frightened animals become scattered and overheated, damaging both the meat products and the health of the herd.

Mosquitos and warble flies do the most mischief to reindeer. During the brief summer heat in which these and other insects multiply, the reindeer become very uncomfortable, or worse. Insects can lay their eggs in the moist nostrils of the reindeer. When the larvae develop they can actually cut off the deer's breathing.

When deer are attacked by adult warble flies they become very hard to handle. Economic loss results from loss of weight, lower meat quality, and holes in the hide caused by emerging larvae. Innoculations are being developed to try and control this problem.

The natural migration pattern of reindeer for getting food helps to bring relief from insects that thrive in the quieter area inland from the coastal areas. To obtain relief, reindeer migrate to a river or coastal waters, or a snowbank if available. High, windy ridges sometimes bring the relief they need.

The coastal area of western Alaska where the reindeer were introduced had an abundance of reindeer moss. In general the moss does not grow where trees are found. It hugs the sparce soil around rocks. It seems to prefer the higher, drier areas of the tundra away from the myriad pools of the lower elevation.

Reindeer have an instinct for returning to the place of their birth. For this reason the spring migration brings the females back to their familiar fawning areas. It is vitally important that the herders preserve these grounds for fawning, and allow sufficient forage for the carriers of the next generation.

Under good conditions, a female will calve each year after reaching maturity in her first year. The gestation period for reindeer is 7 months. After the mating season the bulls isolate themselves from the rest of the herd until sometime in December. By then they have lost their antlers and join the herd as it forages through winter storms.

Female reindeer do not shed their antlers until after giving birth. This gives the female some advantage in claiming the best feeding ground—so she has good nourishment for her young.

All through autumn the fawns are taught to find food on the ground. They sprout antlers but continue nursing until the next mating season.

Reindeer Sled Ride

The following was written by Miner W. Bruce at Teller Reindeer Station, Port Clarence, Alaska, June 30, 1893. The story appears in the 1894 Report on Introduction of Domestic Reindeer into Alaska.

The first thing done with a deer that is to be broken is to teach him to lead with the head-stall or halter on. Afterwards he is fully harnessed and led around in this condition. An old sled-deer is now brought up, and the two are securely tied together by means of ropes extending from the girths as described above. The young deer is placed on the opposite side from that in which the old one is in the habit of working, and when another young one is broken he is usually hitched up with the old one's mate, so that when the two young ones are hitched together they occupy the same position in which they were broken.

They are now ready for the first drive, and if the old one is steady he usually has to drag the young one around or else hold him back. If he is inclined to be frisky, however, and they both take it into their heads to run, there is generally a parrot and monkey time of it, in which the driver has not only his hands full, but his eyes, ears, and nose, and more or less snow is deposited under his clothing as he is being dragged about, completely at the mercy of his team.

It sometimes happens, however, that a young deer will go off on the start as quietly as an old hand at the business; but I have found that, like colts, the best driving team is one that will start off at a rush. When this occurs, if one is fond of excitement, he will find enough to satisfy him before the team has got quieted down.

It is not, however, until the two young ones are considered sufficiently well broken to be driven together that real downright, fine enjoyment is to be had. It is of a kind that intoxicates one and makes his head grow dizzy; that concentrates all his thoughts, if he can be said to have any at such a time, into the single one if, when the deer finally stop, there will be a piece of him left large enough for decent mincemeat.

I have always had a weakness for riding behind a lively team, and my experience with bronchos, Indian ponies, and wild steers dashing across a level stretch of country has afforded sufficient excitement to satisfy me on more than one occasion; but they all fade into insignificance when compared with a ride behind a pair of lively reindeer.

In riding a broncho or Indian pony one realizes that all he has to do is keep his seat in the saddle and he will eventually haul up all right, or, if he is thrown off, he can lie quietly on the ground and think it all over; and in a wagon behind a pair of runaway steers, if killed at all it will probably occur suddenly, and he can take his chances with a broken limb by jumping out. But in driving reindeer the lines, looped over his wrists, make him a secure prisoner, and he is just as certain to continue a part of the load the team will carry until they stop, as the lines are sure not to break, something that rarely if ever occurs.

On the morning of November 6, I experienced my first drive with reindeer. The mercury stood at about zero, and the ground was pretty well covered with snow. In some places a hard crust had formed, and in others lay drifts a foot or so deep, of newly fallen snow, while in spots, where the wind had a little freer scope, mounds or little hillocks among the tundra were entirely bare.

I did not announce my intent to drive alone until the team was all ready to start, and when the Siberians learned my intention they seemed horrified and expostulated with me. I did not see anything so dreadful about it and finally slipped the reins over my hands.

The proper position to assume before mounting a sled is to have it drawn up on the right side of the off deer, the driver to hold that one by the headstall, and when he is all ready, let go, and by lifting up his right leg and dropping down at the same time he is pretty apt to find a seat on the sled, for no sooner does he let go from the deer he is holding than off they go.

I got thus far in the preliminary exercises all right, but in a moment I did not know whether I was on the sled or not, being conscious only of being jerked along at a furious rate, and clouds of snow hurled all about me. For some moments I kept my seat, but suddenly a frozen snowdrift was encountered when over I went, and was dragged through drifts and over frozen heaps until the deer finally stopped from exhaustion.

As soon as I got upon my feet I took a view of my surroundings. I was completely covered with snow, and just over my right temple there was a stinging pain, caused by being struck with one of the runners on the sled. I looked toward the station to see if anyone was coming to my rescue, and saw what appeared to be all the natives from the village watching me, and I thought I could hear them laughing. This settled it, and when the deer were ready I was ready also, and over my leg went and down I dropped, and off we went again with a jerk.

This time the deer made for the direction of the tundra, and when we struck it I felt as if the next moment would be my last. At first the sled ran on one runner; then a slight turn made by the deer threw it over so it ran on the other; then it took a dive forward, the bows striking the feet of the deer, who by this time were as badly frightened as myself, and brought every muscle into play, and for a mile I kept on the sled, but we were traveling with the speed of lightning express. The deer had by this time changed their course and were going in the direction of the station, and, when within a few rods of it, suddenly made a turn, as I thought, to show the natives how easily they could upset me, and I was again dragged through snowdrifts until they stopped from fatigue.

By this time I had got thoroughly worked up, and made up my mind that I would either conquer my team or break something, and started them immediately for another spurt. They appeared as fresh as ever now and took a turn over to the beach, the shores of which were lined with drift logs of all sizes. It was a course of about 3 miles straight away, and as we went, bumping against one log and jumping over another, at a furious gait, I felt that if my neck was not soon broken my legs would be. I managed to keep the sled right side up until we had gone about one-half the distance, when the deer gradually slackened their pace, and for the first time answered to my pulling on the lines.

It now became my turn to do a little forcing, and I belabored the animals with my lines, my whip having been left somewhere in a drift at the outset, until I saw that they preferred a good honest pace to a rollicking gallop.

After allowing them a short breathing spell they started on again like a good sensible pair of reindeer, and for a couple of hours I enjoyed the most pleasant ride I have ever experienced.

In due time we reached the station none the worse for my first ride, except the smarting blow received after my first upset and a little soreness in my limbs and back.

I christened my team "Thomas and Jeremiah" before I turned them over to the herders, and they became my favorite deer and the ones I always drove when I went on a long journey. They never got over their habit of running with me at the start, however; but I soon learned that by keeping well astride the sled with the heels of both feet spread well out ahead of me, I could generally keep the sled right side up, and in soft snow could plow them so deep into it that the deer soon preferred to slacken their pace rather than drag so heavy a load.

Appendix C

Excerpt from the Daily Journal of Teller Reindeer Station

A daily journal was kept by William T. Lopp at Teller Station from July 1, 1894 to August 10, 1894 and by Reverend T. L. Brevig from August 10, 1894 to June 30, 1895. The journal appears in its entirety in the 1895 Report on the Introduction of Domestic Reindeer into Alaska.

July 1, 1894. Southwest wind. Captains Porter, Hagerty, and Robinson came over from the anchorage in a whaleboat to see the herd. Rev. Edson conducted divine service in our schoolroom.

July 2, 1894. North wind. Mr. Willocks, of Pittsburg, PA, visited the station. Captains Mason, Williams, and Townsend, of the whaling fleet, repair the lighter launch and anchor it.

July 3, 1894. South wind. The United States revenue-cutter *Bear* arrived at the anchorage about 5 a.m. and steamed over to the station. Forty-eight deer were landed; also a quantity of cedar lumber and spruce posts; Captain Healy's steam launch towed them ashore on the Pacific Steamship Whaling Company's launch. Dr. Jackson remained on shore over night.

July 4, 1894. The *Bear* dressed ship and saluted in honor of the day. Dr. Jackson took inventory of stock on hand at the station. At 8 p.m. the *Bear* weighed anchor and steamed for the watering place on the south side of the bay.

. . . .

July 6, 1894. The *Bear* leaves the watering place and steams over to the anchorage. Charlie and Mary returned from Point Spencer; they report walrus very plentiful.

. . . .

July 24, 1894. South wind with rain. The *Bear* arrives from Cape Serdze, Siberia, with 38 deer—11 males and 27 females.

. . . .

July 26, 1894. Northwest wind. On invitation from Dr. Jackson, I accompanied him up the lakes in the *Bear's* steam launch, which Captain Healy placed at our disposal; we returned about 5:30, and after taking dinner with Captain Healy, came ashore. A male and female deer which were crippled on ship or in landing, had to be killed. Mr. Grubin and the herders milked two quarts of milk from six deer, two bottles of which were sent to Captain Healy and officers on the *Bear*.

. . . .

July 31, 1894. The *Meyer* beat up closer to shore and employed natives to help discharge the vessel. The Lapps and their baggage were sent on shore. An Eskimo remarked when he first saw the Lapps: "Well, well! These are the people we have seen on our playing cards for all these years." We saw the Lapps milk deer; after lassoing, they make a halter-like noose with which one holds the deer while another milks.

August 1, 1894. Calm, with south wind. Mr. and Mrs. Lopp move into the herders' house and the Kjellmanns into the west end. The Brevigs move into the east end of the frame house. The work of discharging the vessel progresses very slowly. During the night the station dogs broke into the dugout and killed the old goat of the Kjellmanns, and during the day they killed one of the kids.

. . . .

August 6, 1894. Northeast wind. The *Meyer* had discharged her cargo for Port Clarence and Cape Prince of Wales, and commenced to take in a supply of water before leaving. The Gambles remained at the station all day and night. The Lapps drove the deer into a pen to milk them, and obtain about 6 quarts of milk.

. . . .

August 8, 1894. Calm, fine day. The whaler *Fearless* was sighted near land through the fog, and when the fog lifted she anchored near the *Meyer*. Brevig and Gamble boarded the *Fearless* and took dinner with Captain Simonson. In the afternoon Captain Holland and Captain Simonson of the *Fearless* came ashore and visited station and herd. The Gambles went on board the *Meyer* in the evening. The herd was driven into the pen and 83 female deer, 4 sled deer, 5 steers, and 8 bucks were selected and marked as the Cape Prince of Wales herd, the mark being a round

hole in the right ear. Two deer were marked in a different manner for each of the herders.

. . . .

August 11, 1894. Calm, clear, and a beautiful day. The east end of the herders' room was fixed up as a kitchen and storeroom for Brevig, and the west end as a private storeroom for Kjellmann. The herders not with the herd are making gill nets and tents. Traded some salmon.

. . . .

August 13, 1894. Calm, clear, fine day. Early in the morning a steamer was sighted; she anchored close up to shore at 8 a.m. It was the *Albion* from San Francisco with Bruce and Gibson on board with their Port Clarence troupe of Eskimos as passengers. Captain Lundquist said they had landed a cargo at St. Michaels and from here they were going north to Kotzebue Sound to establish a trader's station. Bruce was speaking about getting another troupe with him down on the side-show line next winter.

The *Albion* left at 2:30 p.m. We sent mail with Captain Lundquist.

. . . .

August 22, 1894. Strong wind changing to west and abating during the day. Early in the morning W. T. Lopp's goods were taken on board to be landed at Cape Prince of Wales. The *Bear* sailed at 9:30 a.m. Captain Healy intimated that he might call again. Three Lapps and Eskimos went to get logs for a house up the lagoon. Four Eskimos were sent to the herd and 5 will remain at the station. Six quarts of milk were brought in tonight. The first snow of the season appeared on the mountain tops and high hills.

. . . .

August 30, 1894. Light north wind, with light clouds. The Lapps received provisions for a month. A Cape Prince of Wales canoe arrived with letters from Mr. Lopp, to be forwarded with the *Bear* if it anchored here again. The deer are milked daily, and some cheese is being made.

. . . .

September 3, 1894. Calm and overcast. School commenced with 7 pupils during the day session, and 8 of the herders attended during the evening. The logs for the herders' house, west of the other houses, were put in place.

. . . .

September 6, 1894. The *Bear* was moored outside the station this morning, and Dr. Jackson came ashore at 7 a.m. to get Kjellmann and some Lapps to come on board and land the deer. Johan and Mikkel went on board and landed the deer by throwing them overboard and letting them swim on shore. Thirty-two deer were landed.

September 7, 1894. Calm, cloudy, showers. The Mesdames Brevig and Kjellmann were invited on board the *Bear* for dinner. Dr. Jackson was on shore all day settling accounts with Kjellmann. No school, as the teacher's roof leaked so badly that he had to fix it. In the afternoon the officers of the *Bear* were on shore hunting, and most of them visited the station. The ladies returned home from the *Bear* at 10 p.m. and reported a "splendid time."

. . . .

September 14, 1894. Mr. Kjellmann took the 14 deer back to the Eskimo herd this morning and found they were not missed by the herders. The Eskimos were busy boiling deer meat, and Martin said he had killed a female deer that was sick, but no report had been made to the superintendent. Martin was ordered in to the station to explain matters or pay for the deer and leave. A canoe left for Cape Prince of Wales and letters were sent to Lopp. A clear, nice day; calm.

. . . .

September 16, 1894. Clear, bright. Martin was exonerated from killing the deer. Per Rist had killed her, as she was dying, six ribs having been broken. Frederick Larsen was appointed messenger. He is to leave for the herd about noon and return in the evening with report from the herd. Six deer were reported missing and Antesilook hunting for them. The usual Sunday exercises.

. . . .

September 18, 1894. Clear and nice. Seven Eskimo herders were sent up the lagoon for logs and wood. The roof was laid on the herders' house. Brevig put on double windows and painted the sash and frames. The ever-curious Eskimos painted their artegas, noses, faces, etc., without the use of a brush by pressing them against the newly painted windows. Considerable fish was traded. No report from the deer. (An artega is a waterproof "raincoat" made of larger animal intestines.)

. . . .

September 23, 1894. The storm continues; the wind blew with unusual force about 5 a.m. Wind south to east-southeast, abating toward dark. The usual Sunday service and school. About 5 p.m. Frederick had the mishap to wound both hands by the discharge of his gun escaping by the breach instead of the muzzle. The muzzle was stopped with a plug of wood and a spike so securely wedged in that the firing of the gun could not expel them. His hands were badly torn and blistered by powder. A dressing of arnica and laudanum was put on. Some Cape Prince of Wales people said they had found a dead deer near the inlet into Grantley Harbor; also killed a sick deer that had swollen legs. The meat was already consumed.

. . . .

October 6, 1894. Strong northwest wind, cold and blustering, blowing a gale during the night. Kjellmann and Brevig visited the herd and counted the deer, and from various counts by both it was agreed that the flock contained 440 deer. They were in good condition. It was decided to move to a place about 5 miles up Grantley Harbor, as it was thought the prevailing disease was caused by some herb consumed with the moss.

. . . .

October 15, 1894. Calm, clear; thermometer +20 all day. Per Rist, in going out to the herd with his week's supply on his back, tried to cross the ice on one of the lakes back of the station and fell in. His artega bouyed him up until he reached solid ice.

. . . .

October 28, 1894. West breeze; cloudy, with snow flurries. The usual service and Sunday school. Toward evening Thorwald Kjellmann and I visited the village and entered several houses, and found them much better than we had expected; they were warm and had floors, one bed, and bunks for beds. Thermometer, +8 to +16.

. . . .

November 2, 1894. Strong east wind, 0 to +8. The day opened with a catch-as-catch-can fight between Mary and Nah yuk. Charley tried to mediate peace and was sent sprawling to bed by his "better half," and her opponent sent sprawling to the floor headforemost. All is well with the herd. Wocksock is worse and the Lapps have tried bloodletting, and in the evening a woman from the town tried her bewitching ceremonies on him. He was worse from lying naked on the floor, exposed to a draft. I took my medicines home. The bay is covered with ice.

. . . .

November 24, 1894. Strong southeast wind all night, becoming a gale in the morning; +18 to +22. My stovepipe blew down about 11 p.m., and soon after the cask supporting the station school bell blew over into the ditch. The snow in the ditch saved the bell from being broken; some of the castings are broken. The wind lulled at noon, but now it is blowing harder than ever.

. . . .

November 25, 1894. The storm continued all night; about midnight the house shivered and shook on its foundations. Cleared at 1 p.m. and changed to southwest, veering to southeast again with very strong wind. Thermometer +24 to +28. The usual Sunday service and school.

. . . .

December 2, 1894. North wind, colder, +12 to +2. The usual Sunday service and school. About noon the strong wind broke the ice, and some women out fishing were carried along out toward the sea. Mr. Kjellmann with a crew in the lifeboat rescued them.

. . . .

December 9, 1894. Clear, calm, cold, −14 to −20. The usual Sunday service and school. The leading shaman had a confab with the spirits to-night. He had four fires burning in a square and reposed himself in the middle, groaning and sighing. Four new doctors were with him guarding the fires; Charley was one of them. Thorwald Kjellmann went out there to see the show, and the guards vanished, and he, thinking it was a sick man left there to die, spoke to him, but received no answer. The Lapps were cautioned by Mary not to look toward the fire.

December 10, 1894. Calm and bright, −14 to +20. Charley and Mary inspected Kjellmann's feet and asked if they were not stiff or swollen, because he had spoken to the shaman.

. . . .

December 24, 1894. Light northeast and south wind; clear, nice day; +20 to +30. The station has been crowded with natives all day persisting in seeing everything. At 5 p.m. the doors were opened and the room was soon filled with children and adults. Several songs were rendered, and after a short talk on Christmas, the goody-goodies were distributed. During the day every house in town had received Christmas cheer in the form of "cow-cow" (food).

December 25, 1894. Calm and cloudy. Service in the forenoon. In the evening the Eskimo herders were gathered and some games were played, songs sung, and coffee and tea served. At 8 p.m. a gale blew up from south to southwest, with rain and sleet; +30 all day.

. . . .

January 1, 1895. Calm, clear, bright; −2 to +10. Service for the Lapps. In the afternoon I had five patients, Mrs. Wocksock, Sekeoglook, a boy from Nook covered with sores from the waist down, and a woman from town with a rebellious tooth, which was extracted. Thorwald Kjellmann celebrated his sixty-eighth birthday today.

January 2, 1895. Bright and calm; −4 to +2. School commenced after Christmas, and 29 showed up bright and early to get the biscuit. Two sleds arrived from the lakes for the dance.

. . . .

January 14, 1895. Light northeast-east to southeast wind; −33 to 31. As yet we have not seen a genuine Minnesota cold or blizzard, but live in shaking expectation of seeing one before next May.

. . . .

January 21, 1895. Southeast gale; cloudy, with snow and sleet; +22 to +28. A sewing school for Eskimo girls was begun today with 22 in attendance. Evening school is attended by 4 herders.

. . . .

January 30, 1895. Storming still from north-northeast; clear, but snow flying; 0 all day. All herders and Lapps but Solon, Per, and Ahlook were sent to the herd to help Charley separate his herd today.

January 31, 1895. Clear, snow flying, strong north-northeast wind. Kjellmann left for the herd early this morning and Charley's deer were separated and taken behind the bluff across the bay; 115 deer (15 his private property) were taken, 90 females, 3 sled deer; the rest were bulls and gelding. The south side of the house was now so completely blocked up that a tunnel had to be dug through the bank to get an entrance to the schoolhouse.

. . . .

February 2, 1895. Still storming from north-northeast; clear, but snow flying; doors and windows on the south side of the house were entirely blocked up by snow. Charley and family left about noon. Aslak, Moses, and Ahlook will help him with the deer. Thermometer, −4 to +12.

. . . .

February 22, 1895. Strong north-northeast wind, overcast. The flag was hoisted in honor of the Father of Our Country. About 8:30 Mr. George Johnson, from Unalakleet, with two interpreters, arrived, having made the trip from Charley's place since 8 a.m. They are on a missionary trip through this part of Alaska and will remain here some days. Aslak has found one of the missing deer. Thermometer, +12 to +3.

. . . .

March 20, 1895. Strong north-northeast wind, clear. The deer, a two-year-old gelding, was brought in, killed, and was dressed here and the meat put in the storehouse. The right front hip-joint was dislocated and matter had commenced to form around the joint. Thermometer, −11 to +2.

. . . .

March 30, 1895. Very strong northwest to north-northeast wind, overcast with snow flurries; −22 to −8. Geetaugee was around hunting for four deerskins that had been stolen from him while he was out seal hunting. He suspects Nanugok (the thug) of stealing them. Geetaugee wants to enter a complaint against him when the revenue cutter comes.

. . . .

April 1, 1895. Overcast and calm. The man who shot the stray deer proved to be from Nook. He acknowledged the deed and on being told that he would either have to be put in irons or pay for the deer, promised to pay in

fox skins before the *Bear* came. Two men had helped him eat it, and their names were taken and told to help pay for the meat. He threatened to commit suicide rather than be put in irons. Thermometer −12 to zero.

. . . .

April 3, 1895. Calm, clear. A woman from the lakes came in with a two-months-old baby for treatment; it was covered with sores from poor care and filth. One of the best sled deer broke a foot today, getting entangled in the preceding sled, and had to be killed. Thermometer −12 to +4.

April 4, 1895. Clear, calm; −12 to +4. Martin was very sick with rheumatic pains in the hip joint. Frederick was on the sick list from a boil on the knee caused by a neglected frost sore.

. . . .

April 6, 1895. Variable winds, light, clear, and nice; zero to −14. Nanugok came down from the cape last night, and had, according to hearsay, threatened to kill Geetaugee this morning. Nanugok was up at the station nearly all day and denied having taken the skins. He said he was going to leave in the morning, as the people were talking too much. After supper he went down to the village and was shot through the breast by Geetaugee and buried in a snow bank north-northeast from the village. There was no excitement in the village. The ladies at the station were somewhat excited over the affair; also the Laplanders.

. . . .

April 20, 1895. Calm, clear; +12 to +10. Some Nook people complained that they had nothing to eat and were given some dry tom-cod and oil.

. . . .

May 2, 1895. Clear, calm day; −12 to −30. Mathis Eira arrived from the herd, having been one day and two nights on the way. He reported 65 fawns, of which one was stillborn and one was killed because it had a twin brother, and the mother would only care for one. The third was killed in the herd by being kicked by another deer. The deer are thriving, and the pasturage is splendid. The herd are in a protected place where the winds can not blow. Two cape sleds and Charley arrived toward evening.

. . . .

May 7, 1895. Overcast, with occasional glimpses of the sun. The wind changing from northwest to north-northeast, southeast, back to northeast; +25 to +33. Signs of thawing. Taootuk returned from seal hunting in the night with his wife, but minus all signs of seal. Elektoona went up to the herd with two weeks' provisions for the herd. Taootuk and Martin also went up to stay with the herd. Wocksock and Kummuk came home. Several sleds were on the move toward the sandpit with all their possessions.

. . . .

May 25, 1895. Clear and calm, a very fine day; +50 at noon. Samuel and Taootuk came in from the herd and reported 133 calves born, 122 from old deer and 11 from young fawns.

The herd is now near the foot of Grantley Harbor.

. . . .

June 8, 1895. Calm and foggy, rain and cloudy. The Alaska summer is here in all its abundance of rain and fog. Brevig and Kjellmann returned at 7 a.m. with a log 36 feet long and 14 inches in diameter at the smallest end. Frederick, Aslak, Kummuk, and Wocksock went hunting at 4 p.m., followed by W. A. Kjellmann at 6 p.m.

. . . .

June 22, 1895. Clear and bright, with a light west wind in the afternoon; the sun set at 10:50 p.m. and appeared again at 1:50 a.m. (My watch must be twenty minutes fast.) Kjellmann and party returned at 7 this morning with considerable smelt. Martin, Elektoona, and Sekeoglook came in from the herd at 1 a.m. Grantly Harbor and the north half of the bay is now free from ice.

. . . .

June 26, 1895. Clear and calm; a beautiful day, clouding in the evening. At 5 a.m. some natives came and reported "Umeakburk"; two steamers were nearing the anchorage. A sail was seen toward Kings Island, and during the day two more steamers arrived. Several barrels of tomcod were caught in one draw of the seine last night.

Excerpt from Lopp's Diary on the Point Barrow Rescue

A diary written by William T. Lopp describes the northward reindeer drive to rescue whalers caught in ice off Point Barrow, Alaska, and his return journey to Cape Prince of Wales. Lopp's diary, covering February 3, 1898 to May 5, 1898, was reprinted as The Great Reindeer Drive *by his daughter Katharine and her husband Don Johnson, who kindly gave a copy to me in 1975.*

February 3. SE Wind. 26 Above. Commenced packing sleds early in the morning. Started about 11:30. 18 Sleds, 2 Trains of sled deer. Drive about 7 miles. Camped for the night.

February 4. Beautiful day. Requires until 9:30 to pack sleds, hitch up deer. Leave old cow behind, boys said she would never be able to make the trip. (SE Wind 20 above) Cover about 15 miles. Make very slow progress because of deep snow....

. . . .

February 6. N Wind, mild blizzard. 10 below zero. Perningik and son came into our camp from the coast village of Synazot. We were glad to see them. Lieut. Jarvis decided that he and Dr. Call would leave the reindeer, go to the coast, and travel with dog sled. I helped him arrange with Perningik to go with him as a guide and driver. Sokweena and I took Jarvis and Call to Synazot on reindeer sleds. The trip was disagreeable and Sokweena had much trouble with his trailer deer. At Synazot we found an igloo full of people to welcome us. During the evening I helped Jarvis to arrange for the purchase of a team of dogs and sleds.

. . . .

February 8. Clear, N. Wind. 35 below. Rose early. With all our hurry we were unable to get away before 9 o'clock. 3 Sled deer had strayed. Sokweena went to look for them, 2 or 3 miles to the right of our course. Stanley went back 3 miles for lassoes while we were getting ready. Start the herd ahead. I drive ahead part of the time. Stanley and George were left behind, having some trouble with their trailers. They were not in sight at 12 when we stopped for lunch. Hard bread, chipped frozen butter, and maple syrup for lunch. Send Thomas back for the stragglers. Reach a good camping place and pitch our tents. Send Tautuk back to help along with delayed sled. We make fire in our stove and begin to melt snow for water. 26 Below. One deer which boys were breaking to harness broke away from them and remained behind.

February 9. SW Breeze. 35 below. Start early. We were camped near bottom of big hill, which I think was part of Ear's Mountain. By going around the brow of this hill we gradually reached a high elevation. We had a down grade until we reached an arm of the lagoon known as Shishmaref Inlet. Consult our chart and decide to cross the Inlet to the land northeast of the village of Kegiktuk. We reached this land just after dark and camped for the night. We had made up our minds it would be better for us to follow the coast than to go overland across the tundra. On the latter we could make only about fifteen miles a day, and our 3 hours across the Inlet demonstrated to us that on a lagoon we could drive the herd at the rate of 20 to 25 miles per day. Our boys were all glad to be on seacoast again. Charley sang for first time. We made about 20 miles during the day. Instead of driving some of the sleds ahead of herd all followed the herd closely. We found this a great improvement.

February 10. N Wind. 33 below. Before starting, we talked with some of natives from the village, learned that Jarvis and Call had passed through the village. The natives advised us to follow the lagoon, assuring us what we already knew that there was both moss and wood along its shores. We started across the land expecting to reach lagoon about 3 o'clock without deviating from our course very much. About 3 o'clock the lagoon seemed to be in sight and Charley, Stanley, and George drove ahead and pitched camp on lagoon. Darkness overtook us before we reached it and we were compelled to camp on shores of a dry lake full of grass and no moss along its shores. It was necessary to let the herd go back about 2 miles before moss could be found. We used the fourth sled for fuel. We had already burned three in our drive around Ear's Mountain. Camping after dark is very unpleasant, and generally means a late start in the morning. Made 20 miles during day.

. . . .

February 14. SW Wind. 28 below. After breakfast I took a boy with me and walked out on the ice of the Sound, following the sled tracks of Konok who had crossed from Cape Espenberg on Saturday. Jarvis and Call had gone in a northeasterly direction toward Cape Blossom. I was very much discouraged. The ice looked safe but too rough. In places it was piled in great heaps. I was sure we could never get deer sleds through these ice jams without breaking them. We climbed on a high pile of ice in order to get a better view and saw only these rough ice gorges as far as we could see and in all directions. To try to drive the herd across Kotzebue Sound seemed useless. Return to village, met two of our boys. They had made camp about 2 miles south of village. They discussed the matter of crossing ice with village natives and seemed anxious to try it. They went out on ice in northeasterly direction and decided that we could probably pick our way among ice jams. To cross the ice direct to Cape Kruzenstern should not take more than 1-2 days. To go around Kotzebue Sound it would probably require more than eight days. We put it up to the boys and they voted unanimously to undertake the shortcut. . . .

February 15. N Wind. Clear. 34 Below. Reached the beach about an hour after sunrise. Gave herd a chance to graze before driving them on the ice. Fourteen deer sleds and two dog sleds hauled our camp gear, supplies and moss. We made a start due east to avoid rough ice. Many places we were required to go very slowly. The old man from the village, Tradlook, and grandson followed a short distance and had a ride (their first) on a reindeer sled. As we approached the drift from grounded or stationary ice, we were required to cross what had been a few days before, cracks varying from 1 to 6 feet wide. These were now frozen solid. In places we came to smooth areas of ice which seemed to have been frozen in waves or swells. Our course during the day meandered in so many directions that it was difficult to estimate how many miles we covered toward our goal. . . .

February 16. Roused the boys about 3 o'clock. Weather same. Herd gone. Only sled deer remain. We discover that the tracks start toward north shore, therefore do not worry. Cook breakfast, broke camp, packed sleds and were all ready to start before daylight. The darkness and rough ice prevented. In our efforts to follow the tracks of the deer, we scattered out 100 to 300 yards apart, but were unable to follow them because of the roughness of the ice. When day broke, it became evident that the deer instead of going north had turned south toward the shore from whence we came. Four drivers followed the tracks of the herd while we drove on toward Cape K. They expected to overtake them soon and then catch up with us in an hour or two. They disappeared very quickly. We moved slowly often stopping and resting our deer during the day. About noon we left one of heaviest sleds, knowing that the boys with the herd would pick up our trail and follow us, we left them some hardtack and other food in a small pail which we hung on this big sled. Darkness overtook us and still herders and herd were not in sight. Here we were in what seemed to be the middle of Kotzebue Sound with 13 hungry sled deer, no moss to feed them, and the two dog sleds. We pitch camp get supper ready. Just as we begin to eat the herders come up with the lost herd. There was much rejoicing. . . .

February 17. . . . After waking, walk a mile to Pumeuktuk's house to get one of his boys to carry a letter to Pt. Hope for Jarvis. Pumeuktuk was an old friend. Mrs. Lopp and I had spent several days in his igloo when enroute to Pt. Hope in 1892-3. They explained to me that the baby girl which they were hoping for at that time was another boy. They already had four or five boys in

their family so they swapped this boy baby off for a girl and showed me the girl who was now five years old. . . .

. . . .

February 23. Snowed in. Snowdrifts all around our tent. Wind continues to blow a gale until noon. All our sleds covered several feet in snow. Boys round up the herd, find sled deer fast on account of twisted ropes. Part of the deer had stampeded. Dig out and shift tents. Bertholf pitches his tent and repairs it. Make preparations to start early in the morning. Bertholf to go ahead with his 2 dog sleds and get additional supplies at Pt. Hope, and bring them back to us at the mouth of the Kivalina River.

. . . .

March 2. Weather clear. Two of Nelson's dogs break away and chase the herd three or four miles up a big hill. Wound a cow and calf. We killed a calf, a male deer, and give to Avaluk; also rice, tea, coffee, molasses, and a stove, as pay for going with us as guide across the mountains to Pitmegea Divide. We get very late start, make only 7 or 8 miles, going up the north branch of the Kivalina River. One cow lame—and kill her. Find many acres of bushes along small river. I feel almost sick during the afternoon.

. . . .

March 15. NE Wind. Much snow flying. Try to get P. to go with us with his dog sled, but he said the weather was too bad. He told us we could travel along the lagoon about 4 or 5 hours and strike another point of land jutting out into the lagoon where we would be able to get moss. This was the coldest day I have ever experienced. (Jarvis' thermometer 45 below). It was blowing a gale and the snow was so thick we could not see any distance.

Becoming chilled, I put on a fourth parka, making in all 2 squirrel skin parkas and 2 reindeer parkas. Find one small stick of wood, and a few sticks around an old Indian grave. Camp for the night.

. . . .

March 18. Light NE breeze. Jarvis and driver start back to Dr. Call's camp early in AM. We arrange to meet again at Icy Cape about Sunday, moss and weather. If we pass there first we are to leave a reindeer carcass. We discover that during the night five wolves have killed and eaten an old cow that was lying at edge of herd, only bones and hide left. Travel on the lagoon during day, made fair speed. About sunset, see a pole 4 or 5 miles off and wonder if it is Icy Cape, but we can hardly hope we are so far along. Kill a fawn for food. George and Tantuk stand watch at night to protect the herd against wolves. Think we are almost at the mouth of the Ookootek River.

. . . .

March 30. Clear day. Reach Ignevah 9:30 AM. Wash face. Walk ahaed while they feed dogs. Did not overtake me until had walked 6 or 7 miles. Meet some dirty, sooty-faced sailors with guns, going down to see the reindeer. One walked back with me. He had been out on ice looking for flour, etc. left there months ago when the *Narwhal* burned. I had no dinner, and was nibbling a piece of hard frozen bread. The sailor ate the piece with relish. Met sailors harnessed to sled like dogs. They were after wood. We sight the Barrow village in the distance. Could hardly realize I was nearing my Journey's end. Seemed too good to be true. As I approached could see great strings of what resembled washing hanging out. It was deer and sealskin drying. As we drove along the edge of the village, the natives came out to shake hands with us. Little children came out and insisted on shaking hands. The trail led to Dr. Marsh's house. Jarvis, Call, Doctor and wife were all out to meet me. See myself in glass in Doctor's house first time for weeks. Was hardly recognizable. Walked down through village with Jarvis. Meet McIlhenny and Capt. Aken. Go to Brower's place, see Capts. Porter, Sherman, first mate Ellis, Mesrs. Hobson, Gordon, and Brower. Eat lunch there. Then go to Dr. Marsh's for dinner. Attend prayer meeting that night. About 150 natives present. Songs in Eskimo. Ungrammatical but musical. Many of them lead in prayer. Call on me for a few remarks. Listen attentively but had difficulty in understanding my Cape Prince of Wales dialect. They have very fine faces. The finest average lot of Eskimo I have ever seen together. Shake hands all around at close of meeting.

Endnotes

1. Sheldon Jackson, *Report on Introduction of Domestic Reindeer into Alaska*, 1894, page 19. Jackson was concerned that ownership by white men would completely frustrate efforts to teach the Alaskan people the basics of "civilized" economics.

2. 1898 *Report*, page 24.

3. 1898 *Report*, page 29.

4. 1898 *Report*, page 37.

5. 1900 *Report*, page 24.

6. The number of deer is stated in the 1899 *Report* on page 16. All such numbers in the *Reports* should be viewed as approximations because of the difficulty of making accurate counts under the conditions in Alaska.

7. Cathie Carlisle, "A Light in the Northland," *Lutheran Standard*, March 2, 1984.

8. Henriette Lund, *Of Eskimos and Missionaries*, page 8.

9. 1904 *Report*, page 12.

10. 1906 *Report*, page 61.

11. 1906 *Report*, page 81.

12. Carl J. Lomen, *Fifty Years in Alaska*, page 110.

13. Clarence L. Andrews, *Eskimo and His Reindeer in Alaska*, page 87. Andrews' book tells of the unfair treatment of the Eskimos by some white men. It is also an excellent source of firsthand accounts of Eskimo life as Andrews experienced it.

14. Richard O. Stern, *Eskimo, Reindeer and Land*.

15. Lomen, *Fifty Years in Alaska*, page 87. Lomen does not clarify what is meant by "succeeded." The term usually is linked to inheritance or other means of attaining ownership with no payment involved.

16. Andrews, *Eskimo and His Reindeer in Alaska*, page 145. As I understand it, "open herding" meant that the animals grazed without being herded—only checked on occasionally—then were rounded up for counting, marking, or harvesting. "Close herding" meant 24-hour attendance, usually with three shifts of two herders each. This was the schedule initiated by Jackson with the apprentice training—as patterned after the Laplanders. (Also see Stern, pages 48-49.)

17. Stern, *Eskimo, Reindeer and Land*, page 61. Why Stern refers to "one" Eskimo representative I do not know. In *The Reindeer Problem in Alaska*, Mozee refers to "two."

18. Ben B. Mozee, *The Reindeer Problem in Alaska*, page 21.

19. *Alaska Press*, September 21, 1934.

Bibliography

Alaska 5:3. University of Alaska, Institute of Social, Economic and Government Research.

Alaska. *Report of the Governor of Alaska for the Fiscal Year 1930*. Washington, D.C.: Government Printing Office (GPO), 1930.

Andrews, Clarence L. "Alaska's First Educator." *Alaska Life* (September 1943).

Andrews, Clarence L. *The Eskimo and His Reindeer in Alaska*. Caldwell, ID: Caxton Printers, 1939.

Bigjim, Fred. *Sinrock*. Portland, OR: Press-22, 1983.

Bixby, William. *Track of the Bear*. New York: David McKay, 1965.

Brickey, James and Catherine Brickey. "Reindeer, Cattle of the North." *Alaska Journal* 5:1 (Winter 1975).

Brooks, Maria. "Sinruk Mary: The Reindeer Queen of Alaska." *Northwest Magazine* (September 27, 1984).

Brower, Charles D. *Fifty Years Below Zero*. New York: Dodd Mead, 1952.

Carlisle, Cathie. "A Light in the Northland." *Lutheran Standard* (March 2, 1984).

Cocke, Mary and Albert Cocke. "Hell Roaring Mike: A Fall from Grace in the Frozen North." *Smithsonian* (February 1983).

Cook Inlet Historical Society. *Explorations in Alaska*.

Captain Cook Commemorative Lectures, June-November 1978. Anchorage: Cook Inlet Historical Society, 1980.

Engerman, Jeanne. "Letters from Cape Prince of Wales: A Mission Family in Northwestern Alaska, 1892-1902." *Alaska Journal* 14:4 (Autumn 1984).

The Eskimo 6:4 (January 1940); 7:4 (October 1940).

Hadwen, Seymour and Lawrence J. Palmer. *Reindeer in Alaska*. Bulletin 1089. U.S. Department of Agriculture: GPO, 1922.

Healy, Captain Michael. *Report of the Cruise of the Revenue Cutter Corwin in the Year 1885*. Washington, D.C.: GPO, 1887.

Jackson, Sheldon. "Educational Affairs in Alaska." *Education Report, 1892-1893*. U.S. Bureau of Education: GPO, 1893.

Jackson, Sheldon. "Preliminary Report." *Report of Commissioner of Education on Introduction of Reindeer into Alaska*. U.S. Bureau of Education: GPO, 1890.

Jackson, Sheldon. *Report on Introduction of Domestic Reindeer into Alaska*. 13 volumes. U.S. Bureau of Education: GPO, 1891–1908.

Johnshoy, J. Walter. *Apaurak in Alaska*. Philadelphia: Dorrance, 1944.

Lomen, Carl J. *Fifty Years in Alaska*. New York: David McKay Company, a Division of Random House, 1954.

Lopp, William Thomas. *The Great Reindeer Drive*. Unpublished reprint of diary covering the relief expedition to Pt. Barrow in 1898. Compiled by Katharine and Don Johnson.

Lund, Henriette. *Of Eskimos and Missionaries: Lutheran Eskimo Missions in Alaska, 1894-1973*. No place: American Lutheran Church, 1974.

Miller, Max. *The Great Trek*. New York: Doubleday, 1935.

Mozee, Ben B. *The Reindeer Problem in Alaska*. Pamphlet in Wickersham Collection, Alaska State Historical Library, Juneau, AK. 1933.

Palmer, Lawrence J. *Improved Reindeer Herding*. Circular 82. U.S. Department of Agriculture, 1929.

Phebus, George Jr. *Alaskan Eskimo Life in the 1890s as Sketched by Native Artists*. Washington, D.C.: Smithsonian Institution, 1972.

Reindeer Herders' Association. *Goals and Objectives for the Development of the Reindeer Industry in Northwest Alaska*. GSA Juneau 1311. U.S. Department of Interior, 1979.

"Reindeer Herding: An Industry Revives in the Alaska Bush." *Alaska Journal* 19:3 (Summer 1979).

Seveck, Chester Anakak. *Longest Reindeer Herder*, 12th edition. No place: Rainbow Ventures, 1973.

Stern, Richard O., Edward L. Arobio, Larry L. Naylor, and Wayne C. Thomas. *Eskimo, Reindeer, and Land*. Bulletin 59. Fairbanks: Agricultural Experiment Station, 1980.

Strickland, Dan. "Murder at the Mission." *Alaska Journal*. Volume 16 (1986 composite edition).

Townsend, Charles H. "Notes on the Natural History and Ethnology of Northern Alaska." *1885 Report of Cruise of the Revenue Cutter Corwin*. House Executive Document 153-11. Washington, D.C.: GPO, no date.

U.S. Bureau of Education. *Educational Affairs in Alaska*. Education Report, 1892-1893. Washington, D.C.: GPO, no date.

U.S. Bureau of Education. *Report of the Commissioner of Education, Alaska, 1897-1898*. Washington, D.C.: GPO, no date.

U.S. Bureau of Education. *Work of the Bureau of Education for the Natives of Alaska, 1917-1918*. Bulletin 40. Washington, D.C.: GPO, 1919.

U.S. Department of the Interior, Office of the Secretary. *Survey of the Alaska Reindeer Service, 1930-1933*. Washington, D.C.: GPO, 1933.

U.S. Treasury. Division of Revenue Cutter Service. Document 2101. Washington, D.C.: GPO, 1899.

Updegraff, Harlan. Reprint of Chapter XXVI, *Report on the Alaska School Service and on the Alaska Reindeer Service*. Washington, D.C.: GPO, 1909.

Wells, James K. *Ipani Eskimos: A Cycle of Life in Nature*. Anchorage: Alaska Methodist University, 1974.

Willoya, Emma. Tape recorded interview with Alice Postell, 1979.

Wilson, William H. "Railroad and Reindeer." *Alaska Journal* 10:1 (Winter 1980).

Index

This is a proper name index of persons, groups, and places, as well as ships, laws, and newspapers of particular importance. Because they are mentioned so frequently, Alaska as a place, Eskimos as a group, and Sheldon Jackson are not indexed. Missions and reindeer stations are cross-referenced to commonly used place names where possible (e.g., American Missionary Association Mission at Cape Prince of Wales, see Cape Prince of Wales). The Appendices are not indexed.

A

Acebuk, 55
Agent of Education, 8, 9-10, 17, 60
Agibinik, Esther, 32
Ahlook, 46, 55
Ahmahktoolik, 55
Alaska Native Claims Settlement Act (ANCSA), 51, 86
Alaska Press, 83
Alaska Railroad, 78
Alaska Reindeer Service, 75, 78, 82-83, 85
Alaska Steamship Company, 77
Albert, 55
Albikok, 55
Aleutian Islands, xxii (map), 3, 7, 31, 48, 53, 59
Aleuts, 3, 7, 10, 86
Allokeuk, William, 83
Allokeuk and Konuk Herd, 83
Amaknak Island, xxii (map), 15
Amakravinik, 55
American Missionary Association Mission at Cape Prince of Wales, see Cape Prince of Wales

Amundsen, Roald, 51
ANCSA, see Alaska Native Claims Settlement Act
Andrews, Clarence Leroy, xx, 57, 67, 75, 81, 83
Andrewuk, Mary, 42, 55
Angolook, 55
Anikartuk, 72
Annu, Stephen, 55
Antisarlook, Charley, 27, 32-34, 39, 46, 50
Antisarlook, Mary, 32-34, 50
Arctic Circle, xxii-xxiii (map), 5, 22, 42
Arctic Ocean, xxii-xxiii (map), 4, 8, 17, 31, 48, 56, 58
Athabascans, 86
Avogook, 55

B

Bahr, Aners (Andy) Aslaksen, 38, 76
Barrow, see Point Barrow
Bear, 4, 11, 12, 13, 14-15, 16-17, 19, 20, 27, 28, 31, 48
Belvedere, 33
Benjamin, 55
Bering, Vitus, 7
Bering Sea, xx, xxii (map), 3, 4, 8, 11, 15, 17, 27, 31, 42, 48, 56, 58
Bering Strait, xxii (map), 11, 16
Bertholf, E. P., 31
Bethel, xxii (map), 53, 55
Bettles, xxii (map), 58
Bikongan, 55
Boini, Klemet Person, 38
Bosekop, Norway, 37
Boston, Massachusetts, 77, 80
Boxer, 78
Brevig, Dagny, 48, 72

Brevig, Julia, 24, 45, 46, 48-49
Brevig, Lenore, 48
Brevig, Reverend Tollef Larson, 24, 39, 44-45, 46, 48-49, 60, 72
Brevig Orphanage, 49
Brooklyn, New York, 80
Broun, Heywood, 80
Brower, Charles D., 4, 34
Brown, Sergeant J. S., 8
Bruce, Miner W., 17, 19, 27
Buckland, xxii (map), 73, 77, 80
Burdick, Charles G., 85
Bureau of Education, see U. S. Bureau of Education
Bureau of Indian Affairs, see U. S. Bureau of Indian Affairs
Bureau of Land Management, see U. S. Bureau of Land Management
Burlew, E. K., 82

C

Call, Dr. S. J., 17, 18, 31-33
Campbell, E. O., 60
Campbell, Frank L., 62
Candle, xxii (map), 73
Cantwell, xxii (map), 78
Cape Navarin, xxii (map), 16
Cape Nome, xxii (map), 32-33, 35, 42, 67 (see also Nome)
Cape Prince of Wales, xxii (map), 8, 9, 19, 20-21, 26, 27, 28-29, 32-35, 42, 43, 46, 48, 53, 55, 56, 59
Cape Reindeer Company, 83
Cape Vancouver, xxii (map), 31
Carrook, 55
Catherine II, 7
Chicago, Illinois, 77

Chicago Daily Tribune, 9
Chilkat Pass, xxiii (map), 40
Chilkat River (and Valley), 38
Chirikov, Aleksei, 7
Chukchis (Siberian deermen/herders), 6,
    11, 12-19, 22, 25, 30, 32, 75
Chukchi Sea, xvii, xxii (map)
Churchill, Frank C., xx, 59-62
Circle City, xxiii (map), 38-39
Commissioner of Education, see U. S.
    Commissioner of Education
Congress, see U. S. Congress
Constantine, 55
Cook Inlet, xxii (map), 58
Corwin, 13
Cripple Creek, 50

D

Dannak, 55
Davis, Larry, 86
Dawson, xxiii (map), 40, 41, 42
Deering, xxii (map), 58, 59, 72, 73
Department of Agriculture, see U. S.
    Department of Agriculture
Department of the Interior, see U. S.
    Department of the Interior
Detroit, Michigan, 80
Devore, Lieutenant D. B., 36
Dexter, Mrs., 55
Dieterich, Dr. Robert, xxi, 86
Dutch Harbor, xxii (map), 31
Dyea, xxiii (map), 38

E

Eaton, General John, 45
Eaton Station, xxii (map), 32, 39, 40,
    42-43, 44-45, 46, 53, 55, 58
Egavik, xxii (map), 80
Eira, Mathis Aslaksen and family, 23
Electoona, 46, 55, 65, 66
Elephant Point, xxii (map), 77, 78
Enungwouk, Joseph, 55
Episcopal church, 67
Episcopal Mission at Tanana, see St.
    James Mission
Eraheruk, 55
Eschscholtz Bay, 77
Etuktituk, Robert, 84
Examiner, The, 30

F

Fairbanks, xxii (map), 67, 78

Ferriera, Tillie, see Tillie Ferriera Seveck
Finland, 19
Finmarken, Norway, 22
Finns, 39, 42, 53, 55
Fish Commission, see U. S. Fish
    Commission
Fort Kenai, xxii (map), 7
Fort Lewis, Washington, 73
Fort St. Michael, see St. Michael
Fort Tongass, xxiii (map), 7
Fort Wrangell, xxiii (map), 7, 8, 9

G

Gage, Lyman, 13
Gambell, Dr. Francis H., 43, 45
Gambell, xxii (map), 58, 59 (see also St.
    Lawrence Island)
General Agent of Education, see Agent of
    Education
Gibson, Bruce, 9, 17, 19
Glydon, Minnesota, 21
Golovin (also known as Golovin Bay), xxii
    (map), 27, 39, 40, 42, 46, 53, 55, 58, 59,
    79, 80
Governor of Alaska, 74, 82, 83
Gravel, Senator Mike, 51

H

Haida, 86
Haines, xxiii (map), 37, 38
Hamilton, William, 58, 59, 60
Hamlet, Captain, 60
Harrison Act (1884), 9
Hatta, Per Johannessen, 38
Healy, Lieutenant, then Captain Michael
    A., 8, 11-17, 19, 31
Hecla, 41
Hegness, John, 84
Henry, 55
Howard, General, 8

I

Ibiono, Peter, 55
Icy Cape, xxii (map), 73
Igloo, see Mary's Igloo
Iliamna, xxii (map), 58
Indians, 3, 8, 10, 11 (see also Aleuts;
    and Athabascans, Haida, Kodiaks,
    and Tlingits)
Ingnoven, 55
International Fur Seal Convention (1911), 7
Ipani, 3-6

Iuppik, 27
Ivanoff, Stephan, 55
Iyatunguk, Frank, 55
Iziksic, 27

J

Jarvis, Lieutenant, then Captain D. H., 31-
    35, 49
John, 55
Juneau, xxiii (map), 83

K

Kansas City, Missouri, 80
Kauchak, Frank, 55
Kelly, John W., 30, 58
Kemi, Samuel Johnsen and family, 23
Keok, James, 33, 55
Ketchikan, xxiii (map), 59
Kittilsen, Doctor A. N., 32, 44-45
Kittredge, Nellie, see Nellie Kittredge Lopp
Kivalina, xxii (map), 58, 65, 66, 67, 73
Kivalina River, 66
Kivyeargruk, 33, 55
Kjeldberg, Emil, 38
Kjellmann, Thorwald, 23, 44
Kjellmann, William A., 22-25, 36, 38, 40,
    43, 44-45
Klukwan, xxiii(map), 38
Kobuk, xxii (map), 73
Kobuk River, xxii (map)
Kodiak, xxii (map), 7
Kodiaks, 7
Koktoak, 27, 55
Kotzebue, xxii (map), 42,43, 53, 55, 60, 61,
    67, 73, 80
Kotzebue Peninsula, xxii (map), 82
Kotzebue Sound, xxii (map), 31, 33, 76, 79
Koutchok, Moses, 55
Koyukuk River, xxii (map), 43
Kulana, Alexander, 55
Kuskokwim River, xxii (map), 43, 58

L

Lake Klukshu, 39
Landers, Judge, 60
Lapland, 19, 22, 23, 25, 41
Lapps, xix, xx, 18-19, 22-25, 27, 36-39, 42,
    43, 44-45, 49, 53, 55, 58, 63, 64, 68, 76,
    80, 87
Larsen, Frederik, 23
Lewis, G. 41
Liebes Whaling Company, 34

Lindeberg, Jafet, 42, 81
Liverpool, England, 36
Lomen, Carl, xx, 66-67, 68, 69, 72, 76, 81, 83, 84
Lomen, (Judge) Gudbrand, 66, 83, 84
Lomen and Company, 61, 68, 74, 75, 76-78, 79-81 (see also Lomen Reindeer and Trading Corporation)
Lomen family, xxi, 66-67, 84
Lomen Reindeer and Trading Corporation, 81, 82-85 (see also Lomen and Company)
Lopp, Nellie Kittredge, 20-21, 35
Lopp, William T., 9, 19, 20-21, 26, 28, 33-34, 46, 58, 60, 69, 74, 75
Los Angeles, California, 80
Lund, Dr. C. O., 58
Lutheran church, 48, 51
Lutheran Mission at Teller, see Teller Mission

M

Mackenzie River, xxiii (map), 76
Macon, Georgia, 13
Madison, Wisconsin, 22, 23
Marine Mammal Protection Act (1972), 51
Marsh, Dr. H. R., 34
Mary's Igloo, xxii (map), 67, 69, 72, 73
McCullock, 13
McFarland, Mrs. Amanda, 9
McIlhenny, Mr., 34
Methodist church, 51
Military Department of the Columbia, 8
Miller, Max, 76
Minaville, New York, 8
Minneapolis, Minnesota, 77
Minungon, 55
Moses, 46
Mozee, Benjamin B., 78, 83
Mt. McKinley, xxii (map), 78
Mt. St. Elias, xxiii (map), 7
Munnock, 55

N

Nabactoolik, 76
Nakkila, Mikkel Josephsen and family, 23
Nallogoroak, 55
Nash, Roy, 85
Native Claims Settlement Act, see Alaska Native Claims Settlement Act
Native Reindeer Herders Association, 86
Native Skin Sewers Cooperative, 51
Netaxite, 33

New York, New York, 23, 41, 77, 81
New York State Conservation Commission, 80
Nilima, Alfred, 63, 68
Noatak, xxii (map), 67, 73
Nome, xxii (map), 13, 27, 32, 40-43, 47, 48, 50-51, 59, 60, 66, 69, 73, 74, 77 (see also Cape Nome)
Nook, see Teller
Noorvik, xxii (map), 73
Norge, 51
North Pole, 51
Northwest District, Bureau of Education, 58, 67, 70, 83
Northwest Territory, Canada, 39, 76
Norton Sound, xxii (map), 3, 31, 58
Norway, 10, 19, 22, 36, 41, 42
Norwegians, 19, 39, 42, 45
Nulato, xxii (map), 53, 55
Nunivak Island, xxii (map), 74, 75, 84

O

Office of Indian Affairs, see U. S. Office of Indian Affairs
Oghoalook, 55
Ohbook, 55
Okitkon, 55
Oklahoma City, Oklahoma, 77
Okomon, 55
Okpolick, 65, 66
Olanna, Jake, 86
Onalick, George, 65
O'Neil, David, 41
Oonmookok, 55
Ootenna, George, 33, 55
Oregon Journal, The, 80
Otpelle, 55
Oyello, 46

P

Paneoneo, 55
Panigeo, 55
Parks, Governor George, 82
Penin, 55
Peter, 55
Philadelphia, Pennsylvania, 80
Pilgrim River, 69
Point Barrow, xix, xxii (map), 4, 21, 31, 32, 33-35, 36, 39, 43, 46, 50, 53, 55, 56, 58, 60, 66, 67, 68, 73, 75
Point Hope, xxii (map), 43, 46, 65, 66, 73
Point Rodney, xxii (map), 27, 32, 39, 46
Point Spencer, xxii (map), 16

Port Clarence, xxii (map), 16, 20, 30, 39, 79
Portland, Oregon, 8, 77, 80, 81
Port Townsend, Washington, 30, 31, 38
Post Office Department, see U. S. Post Office Department
Powyun, 55
Presbyterian church, 8-9, 60
Presbyterian Mission at Point Barrow, 46 (see also Point Barrow)
Pribilof Islands, xxii (map), 7, 27
Prince of Wales, see Cape Prince of Wales
Prince of Wales Island, xxiii (map), 7
Putlkinhok, 55

R

Rachford Committee, see Reindeer Appraisal Committee
Redmyer, Hedley E., 38
Reindeer Act (1937), xix, 85, 86
Reindeer Appraisal Committee (Rachford Committee), 85
Reindeer Council, 83
"Reindeer Queen," see Antisarlook, Mary
Reindeer Service, see Alaska Reindeer Service
Reindeer Transportation Company of Vancouver, 41
Reliance, 8
Revenue Cutter Service, Revenue Marine Service, see U. S. Treasury Revenue Marine Service
Rist, Per Aslaksen, 23
Robert, 55
Roosevelt, President Theodore, 54
Rorondelel, John, 55
Russia, 7, 12, 41, 53

S

Sagoonuk, 55
Sailor's Home, San Francisco, California, 24
Sakpillok, 55
Sami, see Lapps
San Francisco, California, 13, 16, 20, 23, 24, 30, 80
Santa Claus, 80-81
Scroggs, J. G., 41
Seal Islands, see Pribilof Islands
Sea Mammals Act (1971), 4
Seattle, Washington, 21, 24, 37, 38, 41, 46, 59, 66, 76, 77, 80, 81
Secretary of State, see U. S. Secretary of State

Secretary of the Interior, see U. S. Secretary of the Interior
Secretary of the Treasury, see U. S. Secretary of the Treasury
Secretary of War, see U. S. Secretary of War
Segevan, 55
Seim, Conrad, 30
Sekeoglook, 45, 55
Selawik, xxii (map), 73
Sepillu, 55, 60
Serawlook, 55
Seveck, Chester Asakak, 65, 66-67, 68, 73
Seveck, Helen, 67
Seveck, Tillie Ferriera, 66
Seward Peninsula, xvii, xx, xxii (map), 16, 36, 40, 48, 53, 68, 79, 82, 83, 86, 87
Shields, Walter C., 50, 66, 67-68, 69, 70-71, 73, 75, 79, 80
Shishmaref, xvii, xxii (map), 58, 72, 73
Shishmaref Herd, 83
Shoudla, 55
Siberia, xix, xxii (map), 11, 12-16, 27-30, 41, 45, 48, 58, 75,
Siberian deermen/herders, see Chukchis
Sinnock, John, 83
Sinruk, xx, xxii (map), 32, 84
Sinruk Mary, see Antisarlook, Mary
Siquenuk, Thomas, 69
Siri, Hans Andersen, 38
Siri, Per Nilsen, 38
Sitka, xxiii (map), 7
Skagway, xxiii (map), 38, 41
Snake River, 40
Society of Friends, 60
Sokwena, 33, 55
Somby, Aslak Larsen and family, 23
Soovawhasie, 27
Stevens, Senator Ted, 51
St. James Mission (Episcopal Mission at Tanana), xxii (map), 27, 46
St. Lawrence Bay, xxii (map), 30
St. Lawrence Island, xxii (map), 3, 53, 55, 59, 60, 82 (see also Gambell)
St. Louis, Missouri, 80
St. Michael, xxii (map), 17, 27, 31, 36, 42, 46, 75
St. Paul, 7
St. Paul, Minnesota, 24, 77
St. Peter, 7
St. Petersburg, Russia, 7
Strong, Territorial Governor, John F. A., 74
Stuk, 33
Superintendent of Education for Alaska Natives, 21
Sweden, 19, 36, 41

Swedes, 19
Swedish Evangelical Mission at Golovin Bay, see Golovin

T

Tacoma, Washington, 73
Taktuk, 55
Tanana, see St. James Mission
Tanana River, xxii (map), 39
Tatpan, 55
Tautook, 32, 45, 55, 69
Teller (formerly Nook), xxii (map), 39, 59
Teller, Secretary of the Interior, then Congressman Henry M., 10, 17
Teller Mission, 39, 45, 49, 50, 72, 79 (see also Teller Station)
Teller Mission Reindeer Company, 84
Teller Station, xxii (map), 16-17, 19, 20, 24, 25, 26-27, 30, 32, 35, 39, 42, 43, 44-46, 48-49, 52, 53, 55, 58, 59, 79, 80, 83 (see also Teller Mission)
Teller Orphanage, see Brevig Orphanage
Thetis, 13, 59, 60
Thleheena River, 38
Thomas, Dana, 60
Thornton, Harrison, 20
Thornton, Mrs. Harrison, 20-21
Tlingits, 86
Toktuk, 55
Tommy, 55
"Tom the Good," see Lopp, William T.
Tongass, see Fort Tongass
Tornensis, Johan Speinsen and family, 23
Townsend, Charles H., 11
Truman, President Harry, 51
Tungwenuk, Louis, 83
Tununok, xxii (map), 31
Tuttle, Captain Francis, 31, 33

U

Umatilla, 24
Unalakleet, xxii (map), 32, 39, 42, 53, 55, 56
Unalakleet River, 45
Unalaska, xxii (map), 13, 17, 31, 86
Ungawishak, 55
University of Alaska, Agricultural Experimental Farm, Fairbanks, 78
University of Alaska, Institute of Arctic Biology, xxi, 86
Updegraff, Harlan, 64
U. S. Bureau of Education, 12, 21, 28-29, 64, 65, 66, 67, 68, 74, 78, 82

U. S. Bureau of Indian Affairs, 86
U. S. Bureau of Land Management, 82
U. S. Commissioner of Education, 11, 12, 45
U. S. Congress, xx, 9, 12, 22, 27, 54, 57, 60, 61-62, 85
U. S. Department of Agriculture, 66, 72
U. S. Department of the Interior, xx, 12, 26, 39, 59, 75, 82, 86
U. S. Fish Commission, 11
U. S. Navy, 14
U. S. Office of Indian Affairs, 83
U. S. Post Office Department, 43
U. S. Secretary of State, 12
U. S. Secretary of the Interior, 12, 17, 36, 54, 62, 64, 82, 83, 84-85
U. S. Secretary of the Treasury, 13, 31
U. S. Secretary of War, 36
U. S. Treasury Revenue Marine Service, 4, 7, 8, 13, 14, 49
U. S. War Department, 7, 39

V

Valley City, Indiana, 20

W

Wainwright, xxii (map), 56, 57, 67, 73, 75
Wales, see Cape Prince of Wales
War Department, see U. S. War Department
Waseby, 55
Washington, D. C., 9, 12, 59, 62, 82, 83, 84
Wave, 77
Wein Airlines, 67
Weyiouanna, Alex, xvii
Weyiouanna, Elsie, xvii
Widstead, J. C., 44
Willamette Valley, Oregon, 75
Willoya, David, 50
Willoya, Emma, 49, 50-51
Willoya, Mike, 50
Wilmington, North Carolina, 21
Wocksock, 45
Wrangell, see Fort Wrangell

Y

YMCA, Portland, Oregon, 8
Yukon River (and Valley), xix, xxii-xxiii (map), 3, 17, 27, 36, 38-39, 40, 41, 42, 43, 48, 58, 76